FULL CIRCLE

The Real Story Behind My Fairy Tale

Dee Dee Hixson

iUniverse, Inc.
Bloomington

Full Circle
The Real Story Behind My Fairy Tale

iUniverse books may be ordered through booksellers or by contacting:

iUniverse
1663 Liberty Drive
Bloomington, IN 47403
www.iuniverse.com
1-800-Authors (1-800-288-4677)

ISBN: 978-1-4759-8744-7 (sc)
ISBN: 978-1-4759-8743-0 (hc)
ISBN: 978-1-4759-8742-3 (e)

Library of Congress Control Number: 2013907262

Printed in the United States of America

iUniverse rev. date: 5/15/2013

For
Dale—my blessing,
Amy—my strength,
and for
Bethany—my angel

Dedicated to
Big Red

This memoir is based on my own recollection of events; conversations and actions have been portrayed as accurately as my memory allows, with an eye toward giving readers the main concepts. Any errors or omissions are mine. Some names have been changed.

CONTENTS

PROLOGUE

In October of 2003, I danced with my son, Dale, at his wedding. It was a miracle. This was not the kind of miracle where one of us got up out of a wheelchair and against all odds walked across the room. This was a miracle of faith, hope, endurance, patience, and unwavering love. This was a true-life fairy tale.

Around us, the crowd talked and laughed, watched the newlyweds dance, and enjoyed this special occasion. I was in a daze, wandering around the catering hall, looking at people I'd never met before. The crowd jostled me, and I had to make an effort not to veer away and sit in a corner. Occasionally reality would hit me, and I would pinch myself to make sure this was really happening.

Dale and his bride, Rachel, were married on a beautiful fall day overlooking a lake in the desert north of Phoenix. The sun was setting, spreading stunning pink and purple rays on the high thin clouds. He was handsome in a solemn black tuxedo, she was beautiful in her white gown, and the simple ceremony was lovely.

Afterward, we went to a reception in the lodge, where I only knew a handful of people: my mom, my sister and brother, my daughter and grandsons, and Steve, my ex-husband. There were some awkward moments.

As we walked up to an old friend of his, Dale greeted her and said: "Barbara, I want you to meet Steve and Dee Dee, my parents."

"Wait, what?" Barbara looked at us, confusion in her eyes. She motioned to Roy and Pat, who she knew as Dale's parents. "Aren't Roy and Pat ...?"

"These are my biological parents, and we've just recently gotten to know each other." Dale smiled, trying to smooth things out, not for the first time or the last. He spent a lot of that evening explaining Steve and I to people.

I had only known my son Dale for four months. When Dale and Rachel started planning their wedding, he never dreamed he would have a whole new family to deal with, or how confusing his life was about to become. (Figuring out family photos for the wedding was very bizarre.)

At the end of the night, Dale walked over to my table. He looked so wonderful—tall, handsome, and strong—so much like my father. "May I have the last dance?" he asked and bowed graciously over my hand. Tears started streaming down my face— again. This handsome young man, my son, was back in my life. I cried through the entire dance.

Thirty-seven years before, I had handed my newborn baby over to strangers. They gave him to a family to love and raise as their own. Back then, in 1966, it never entered my mind that I would get to be a part of my son's wedding. Yet here we were.

On a magical night, I danced with my son, Dale, at his wedding. It was a miracle.

CHAPTER ONE

1965 Steve

I was (still am) the good girl. I was the one who got good grades, didn't get in trouble, did was I was supposed to; you know, "the good girl." Yet somewhere along the way, I got wired to believe that I wasn't quite good enough. Not as pretty as my cousin Carolyn, not as smart as Gretchen, not one of the cool kids. I was on the honor roll in high school but afraid to go to college. I didn't know I was smart and was afraid I would fail. It took me many, many years to figure out that wasn't true.

My older brother, Ronny, was the bad boy. He was always in trouble. He struggled in school and drove my parents sick with worry. There were cops at the door in the middle of the night and parties every time my parents went out, with me cleaning up the mess so he wouldn't get caught and I didn't get beat up. In March 1965, Ronny had nearly forty high school buddies over to our house once when Mom and Dad were out. They'd broken two lamps and trashed the kitchen by the time I got home from volleyball practice.

"Ronny! You've got to get them out!" I yelled.

Ron was a little drunk and just grinned at me. His hair was disheveled, and his eyes were reddened. "Oh, we're just having some fun," he said. "Don't be such a Goody Two-shoes."

Without a word I started cleaning up the kitchen, pushing kids out of my way, and filling up trash bags with empty beer bottles, paper plates, and cups. Cleaning up was to become a theme in my life.

I also had two younger brothers and a sister: Terry, Shelley, and Jeffrey. As they didn't come along until several years later, they were always "the little kids," and I was the one taking care of them when my mom was busy. I was a caregiver from my early days, groomed to put other people's needs ahead of my own.

All of my mom's family was Mormon, and we grew up in the church. We lived in Tempe, Arizona, which was a very small college town back then. My parents would drop us off at Sunday school every week, and afterward we would walk to the local drug store for a treat. The owner would see all five of us traipse in and jump up on the bar stools at the counter. He always knew we wanted cherry fizzes, and he had them ready for us. After a while, Mom would come pick us up. I think she must have loved those few hours of peace and quiet on Sunday mornings. She didn't work when we were little, but she certainly had her hands full with five kids.

My dad owned an aviation business and worked long hours. One of our fun treats was going to the airport with him on Saturdays and playing in the airplanes he was servicing or repairing. We would crawl up in the cockpit and have great imaginary escapades. The boys were famous fighter pilots, of course. Shelley and I became famous female pilots flying around the world, having adventures, falling in love. Typical kids' fantasies.

Dad was also a private pilot, and our biggest thrill was flying with him on the weekends. We had great adventures as he flew us around the state. The best time was when Dad took just me on a trip to Tucson or somewhere in northern Arizona. It was our special time together. One of my favorite times was when he took me, my mom, her mom, and her grandma on a flight around the city. My great-grandmother was ninety-two years old, and it was her first time in an airplane. A photographer from the newspaper was there, and we were in the Sunday paper—four generations of women flying together. That was really special; I still have that photo.

● ● ●

In 1965, I was seventeen, a senior in high school, and learning to navigate the world as a teenager in the turbulent sixties. I wore my hair in a smooth bob, finally had contacts so I didn't have to wear my glasses all the time, and was the good student, always trying to do the right thing.

And then I fell in love with Steve. He was cute! Maybe a little short, but he had beautiful dark eyes, longish, wavy brown hair, and a great smile. All the girls thought Steve was adorable. He was only a junior, but that didn't matter. He was fun and popular, and I couldn't believe he was interested in me.

We started dating, and I was one happy girl. We'd pull up to the Dash Inn in his shiny red Ford Ranchero—one of those very cool cars with a pick-up bed in the back—and I thought I was in heaven. (The Dash Inn was the local burger joint and was the first place in town with a drive-through). Even better was when he would let me borrow his Ranchero. I'd go pick up a couple of

girl friends, and we'd zoom past the Dash Inn running the gears.
We felt so cool!

Steve's and my relationship grew quickly, and by the time I
graduated from high school, we were crazy about each other. We
were so young. At seventeen, why don't you realize how much
life is still ahead of you? How much you still have to learn about
yourself and the world? I saw our future with the whole married-
with-children, white-picket-fence, dog-running-in-the-yard,
happily-ever-after thing going on.

I couldn't have been more wrong.

Several weeks after my high school graduation, Steve convinced
me that if I truly loved him, I would prove it. It was not a beautiful
experience. We had been together for about six months and spent
a great deal of our time fighting the temptation to go all the way.
Well, I was doing the fighting. He was doing the tempting, and
the persuading, and the pleading.

Fourth of July weekend, I finally gave in. We were parked out
in the desert, both of us hot and sweaty and cramped in the back
seat of his little tiny car, making out. As things progressed, we
started trying to figure out how to get all our limbs in the right
place without breaking something. I was crazy about him, and
before I knew it, our clothes were off and there was no stopping
us.

In the midsixties, no one carried condoms around with them,
and although the famous "pill" was starting to be available, it was
not an option for me. I didn't do that. After all, only slutty girls
planned ahead to have sex. But we were full of heat and lust, and I
knew I was being bad, but now he would really love me forever.

When it was over, the realization of what I'd done hit me,
and I was really upset. Steve held me, and he told me he loved me

and everything would be okay. When he finally took me home, I snuck into the house, washed the blood off my underwear, and called him. We talked about what had happened while I cried until the wee hours of the morning.

"I was raised to be a nice girl who didn't do those things," I said as I sobbed. "I'm going to go straight to hell."

"It'll be okay, honey," Steve reassured me. "We're going to be together because we love each other. It will turn out fine."

Besides the guilt, several weeks later I also discovered that I suffered from fertility. Yep, one time only, and my period was late. Of course my mom had warned me. She had pounded it into my head, but I just knew it wouldn't happen to me.

Right.

I was horrified and sick with guilt and worry. *How could this possibly happen? Why me?* When I was a few days late, I told Steve.

I could tell he was as scared as I was. "Don't worry, honey." His reassurance didn't keep my hands from trembling (or his hands from wandering). "Don't worry, I'm sure nothing's wrong."

After a week went by and still no period, I was beside myself with fear. By the time two weeks went by, I was convinced. There were no at-home pregnancy tests in those days, and I was afraid to make a doctor appointment by myself. My parents were up at their cabin in the mountains near Payson, so at least my mom wasn't around to witness my hysteria. The days kept going by, and Steven and I finally knew there was a pretty darn good chance I was pregnant. Steve was getting ready to start his senior year of high school, and neither of us was prepared for the consequences we were about to face. We cried and fought and consoled and talked about it for hours and hours.

One night after we'd been out to a movie, we stood next to Steve's car in front of my parents' house having yet another conversation about what we should do. Steve had his arms wrapped around me as we stood there, and then he stepped back and took both of my hands in his. He kissed me very gently and said, "Dee Dee, I want us to get married."

I loved him so much at that moment and was so tempted to say yes, but even at seventeen I was smart enough to know the odds were heavily stacked against a high school marriage. How would we support ourselves and a baby? He still had his senior year ahead of him. Abortion was out of the question, as this was long before abortion was legal, but that wasn't the real problem. It was just something I couldn't do. I was too scared, and it seemed so wrong to me.

We parted that night with no clear plan in place. I was just floating on a bed of anxiety and fear, my thoughts running around and around in my head.

Telling my parents was the hardest thing I'd ever done. One day in early August, my mom called from the cabin just to check in. The cabin was just a few hours away, and I tried to drive up a couple of times a month, but I'd been making excuses and hadn't been up for a while. I was supposed to go and see them the coming weekend, but I just wasn't ready to face them.

While we were talking, I told Mom I needed some help with something. "Mom, I can't break a confidence, so don't ask me who, but I think one of my girlfriends might be pregnant and she doesn't know what to do. What should I tell her to do?"

Mom hesitated for a while and then said, "Is this someone I know?"

"Yes, but I'm not telling you who. I just need to help her."

Mom said, "Well, the first thing she needs to do is tell her mother so she can get a doctor appointment and find out for sure. Dee Dee, she has to talk to her parents right away."

"She's too afraid of what they'll say," I cried. "Mom, she's scared to death."

"I'm sure she is, but she needs to tell someone who can help her."

"Okay, thanks Mom. I'll tell her what you said." I replied and then made an excuse to get off the phone as fast as I could.

Oh, please. Is there a parent out there who would fall for that? I don't know why I thought I could make her believe me. I guess I was hoping she'd say that being late was normal and not to worry about it.

●　　　●　　　●

In early September Mom and Dad came home from the mountains for a weekend to take care of some business. By this time I was probably about six weeks pregnant, and there was no wishing it away. Steve and I had been out one evening and had yet another long conversation about what to do, and this time we finally made some important decisions. He took me home about ten o'clock, and I went in to tell my parents. He drove home to have the same conversation with his parents.

Mom and Dad handled it as well as any parents could, I guess. I remember lots of tears from my mom and yelling from my father, not to mention the guilt and the shame I felt as they sat there in shock. Mom eventually told me that when they came home from the cabin, she went into the bathroom cabinet and counted the sanitary napkins and realized none were missing. I never thought about that. Can you imagine how awful that must have been for her? Suspecting your "perfect" daughter is pregnant and waiting to find out? In the sixties, the biggest focus was on how to keep the secret so I didn't embarrass the family. Mom couldn't possibly let her friends know what kind of daughter she had. Only bad girls went all the way. Surely getting pregnant was a punishment from God.

The night we told our parents that I was pregnant, Steve and I had made the decision to give our child up for adoption no matter what they wanted, and we were going to stand by that decision. We went round and round with it, and we felt it was our only choice. I would not have an illegal abortion, I knew we shouldn't get married, and in those days, you just didn't keep the child, so adoption was it. We did not waver from our choice. We also made a vow to honor our commitment to not interfere in this child's life.

There were no open adoptions in those days. All the records were sealed, and there were never arrangements for the birth parents to be part of the child's life. We decided to give our baby up because we truly believed he or she would have a better life. We could not change our minds somewhere down the line. It was heartbreaking to come to this decision, but keeping him wasn't right for any of us, and we believed we were doing the right thing.

I was working for a collection agency at the time, so we told everyone that I got a job transfer to Tucson, a couple of hours away. In reality, arrangements were made for me to go to Florence Crittenton Home for Unwed Mothers. Florence Crittenton was exactly as the name says, a halfway house of sorts where single women went to hide from the world while they awaited the birth of the baby they would not raise. You didn't actually move into

Florence Crittenton until you were in your eighth month, so before moving into their facility, they arranged for me to live with a family on the other side of town.

It was the start of a new phase of my life, one that no one could have been prepared for.

CHAPTER TWO

1965–66 The Baby

On the day I moved, my mom was supposedly driving me to Tucson to get settled in my new apartment. Instead we went to downtown Phoenix and had lunch and then went to a movie theater and saw *The Sound of Music*. (I've never been able to watch that movie since.) Then she took me to meet my temporary family, the Smiths, who would take care of me until I was ready to go to "the home." I was just a kid, and I was so scared. It was hard to stand in the driveway and watch her drive away and leave me with strangers. I can't imagine how hard it was for her.

I lived with the Smith family: a mom and a dad with two young children, a boy and girl, both under the age of five. I stayed in a guesthouse that had been converted from a detached garage. It was small but comfortable, a studio with a compact kitchen and tiny bath. It was connected to the house by a walkway, so I had my own entrance and a little privacy when I needed it. And boy, did I need it.

What a great scam that turned out to be. My duties were to get the kids up, feed them breakfast, and make sure they got off to school. Then I took care of them after school, as well as prepared their dinner, gave them a bath, and got them to bed; basically, I was a nanny. That was fine, except that Mrs. Smith thought it would be good for me to do all the laundry and cleaning, scrub the floors, and also be their maid.

I lived with them for about four months in late 1965 and worked my butt off. Steve visited as often as he could and offered as much support as a seventeen-year-old high school senior could. The Smiths did not approve of him coming over, and I don't think he was supposed to. There were very strict rules, but he would sneak in the guesthouse at night a couple of times a week. Someone from Florence Crittenton would come visit periodically and check on me, and I finally started complaining about my workload. When they realized how much the Smiths were stepping over the line and working me so much, I was removed from their home. Scrubbing the floors on my hands and knees every day was not supposed to be in the game plan.

●   ●   ●

So I moved into the Crittenton facility about four weeks ahead of schedule. Interestingly enough, I remember my time at Crittenton as happy. Maybe it was because the girls were all there for the same reason—a sorority of girls and women of all ages and circumstances. We all had big bellies and stories to tell and babies we were going to give away. We were all scared. We cried together and laughed together and commiserated about our problems.

There were usually four of us in one bedroom, and after lights-out, we would whisper our stories to each other. Terri was just thirteen and had run away from a foster home. She was hard and tough; she smoked and talked about living a life I couldn't begin to imagine. Judy was in high school and thought she was in love with her boyfriend until he found out she was pregnant. He dumped her and wouldn't admit he was the dad. Her parents turned away from her as well, so she was really alone.

Then there was Betty, who was forty years old! Ancient to many of us. She kept to herself and didn't talk to us much in the beginning, but we were all so curious. Finally she told us that this was her third child, and her husband had walked out on her. Her grandparents were taking care of her two babies, but she had no means to support any of them, so she had to give this one up.

Everyone had a different story. All the stories were all pretty sad, yet we managed to keep our spirits up somehow.

During the days, the younger girls had high school classes. There were additional classes we could take as well, and chores to do, plus counseling and birthing classes to attend. At night we learned to knit, watched TV, and waited for someone's boyfriend to sneak pizzas over the fence. There are moments I can vividly see some of us sitting in the big community room knitting and watching TV, and then the rest gets very foggy. Every few days, someone would go to the hospital to deliver her baby, and we would never see her again. That was hard for us, because we did bond and become friends. Then they were gone. We weren't supposed to know each other's last names, and I suppose most of us really wanted to leave that time behind us once we rejoined our normal life.

I've often wondered what happened to some of the girls who were there with me. I wonder if any of them ever found their children later in life.

●   ●   ●

One night, just before my due date, we were all sitting around knitting and watching TV late in the evening. I hadn't been feeling well, and my back was killing me. I went to bed around midnight but just could not get comfortable. I dozed for a while and woke up an hour or so later in excruciating pain. This was not just uncomfortable—this was a hard tightness in my stomach, and it felt like there was a knife stabbing me in my lower back. We had all taken childbirth classes, but I was not ready for what was to come in the next few hours. Since we never got to see each other after giving birth, we never heard stories from the other girls about what to expect.

I got up and slowly walked down the hallway until one of the nurses saw me. She took me into the nurse's office and checked me and realized I was in early labor. I was scared to death and in so much pain I thought I would die. She called the hospital and told them to send the ambulance. Sometime in the middle of the night, I was taken to St. Joseph's hospital

I was all alone in a cold, sterile hospital room in the middle of the night and so frightened. There was no one there to coach me or to hold my hand, to tell me they loved me, or to help me through the labor. Every few minutes, a nurse would come in and check on me, but they were always very clinical and cold. I just wanted to make it stop hurting, and there was no one that cared. To them this was just another baby being delivered. This was not a family being started. I felt like I was in to have a tumor removed. It was painful and it was terrifying.

The night dragged on. Finally a doctor came in. "Okay," he said. "I think it's time."

On the morning of April 4, 1966, I gave birth to a baby boy. They immediately took him away and put me in another room by myself. I was hurting, I was lonely, and I was scared. *Oh my God, why didn't someone warn me how horrible this was going to be?*

I think my parents came to see me that next morning, but I'm not even sure. I remember Steve telling me he got a phone call during dinner that evening to let him know that he was a father of a child he would never know. I don't know who called him, or why it was so much later when he found out. All I knew was that he wasn't with me. No one was with me. I was in the hospital by myself for two days. Nurses would check me, someone would bring food, and somehow the hours would pass.

On April 6 several strangers came in my room with the legal adoption documents. Steve was there, and we listened while they told us that there was a family waiting for our baby. As soon as we signed him away, I could go home. At that moment I was ready to change my mind and take him home with me and figure out the details later. They explained that this was a closed adoption and the records would be sealed for ninety-nine years. This was a final decision. With tears rolling down my face, I signed the documents with a shaky hand. Steve was crying also. We just held each other, reassuring ourselves that we were doing the right thing for this baby.

Once the documents were signed, a nurse came in. "You can see the baby for about twenty minutes if you want to."

Steve wasn't sure, but I was. I needed to see him and explain things. A few minutes later, that nurse walked in and handed me this little baby with dark hair and loud lungs. As she put him in my arms, all I could think was, *This beautiful little boy is my son, and I just signed papers giving up all my rights to see him grow up. How can I possibly walk away from him? Is it too late to change my mind?* This was a real baby. We both held him and cried all over his little head, and then all too soon a nurse came in and took him away.

It was heartbreaking, and I was devastated, but there was no going back. Later that day Mom came and got me from the hospital. She took me to a friend's house where I would live for the next month or so, because I certainly couldn't go back home until my belly went down.

● ● ●

Those first months afterward were extremely difficult. I was sad, lost, and alone. I spent my days trying to figure out how to adjust to my life, to cope with so many emotions that plagued me, and to fight off the emptiness that enveloped me. I spent most of my day crying. I missed my baby, I missed my family, and I missed my friends. How was I going to come back and start over and keep this secret?

The days were long; I didn't have a job yet, so I had nothing to fill the time. My girlfriends would call, but I couldn't talk to them without crying. I just told them that Steve and I were having problems. At this point everyone thought I was still working in Tucson, so I had to keep up the charade. I was determined to not let anyone know what a horrible person I was. What I should have done was get some kind of counseling to help me understand and cope, but that was not the thing to do in the sixties. I just had to get tougher and put it behind me. As much as I wanted to hold that baby in my arms during those awful days when I was hiding and recovering, I knew we had done the right thing. I have never regretted the decision to give this baby up for adoption, but it did leave a huge hole in my heart.

Steve and I had spent a lot of time dealing with the pregnancy and what it was doing to us, but we had not given any thought to how we would handle our relationship after the baby was born. He was now a senior getting ready to graduate from high school, and I had been out of his daily life for many months. He was having fun and enjoying his senior year, and I was not a part of it.

When he went to his senior prom, I was still in hiding and could not go with him. He told me he went alone, but I didn't believe him. Who goes to prom without a date? On the last day of school, there was a huge party at the lake. I didn't go. Our worlds started growing apart. When I did see him, I cried a lot. It was awkward to be together, and it was hard to be apart. He wanted to put all of this behind him, and I couldn't let go. We started seeing less and less of each other, which only added to my heartbreak.

It looked like my dream of happily-ever-after was leaving, and I didn't know how to dream again.

CHAPTER THREE

1967–68 Battles

After the baby was born and I returned home, my relationship with Steve was anything but smooth. By early 1967, I had finally gotten back on my feet with a decent job, and I moved into a very small one-bedroom apartment. I needed to be out of my parents' house, because every time Steve showed up or I mentioned his name, my mom went up in smoke. She and my dad wanted me to have nothing to do with him, so having my own apartment was great. But Steve and I fought all the time. We were on for six months, off for three, on again, off again; it was bumpy, to say the least.

One day, just about a year after the baby was born and during one our "off" periods, Steve called to tell me he had been seeing someone else. This wasn't surprising, since the last time we had broken up, we both declared we were done for good. But then he dropped the bomb: after six weeks together, he was giving this girl a ring. He was engaged. *Engaged? Where did that come from? That can't be right.* We were broken up and we fought all the time, but I loved him and he loved me. How could he get engaged to someone else in six weeks?

I was hurt, angry, and heartbroken. I was sure he still loved me, but the emotion of the past year wouldn't leave us. We just didn't know how to deal with it.

I, of course, knew he was making the biggest mistake of his life but could do little about it. I made it a point to find out who this girl was: Joanne from the beauty salon. Then I knew for sure this engagement was a disaster. What did he see in her? She worked at the same salon as Steve's mom; that's how he met her. I'll have to admit Joanne was cute, but how could this have happened so quickly? Steve's mom knew they were dating, and she wasn't so happy about it either. She and I were still close, and she too was sure Steve was making one big mistake.

I spent the next six weeks in total misery. I made too many phone calls to scream and yell at Steve and tell him how much I still loved him. He finally stopped taking my calls. Then late one Saturday night, Steve called.

"Uh, I need to talk to you. Is it okay if I come over?"

I was really surprised to hear from him, but I wasn't strong enough to say no. I told him to come over to the apartment. When I answered the door, Steve stood there and slowly put out his hand. In his palm was an engagement ring. I just looked at him, confused and not knowing what to say.

"The engagement is off. Could we just go for a drive and talk?"

It was once again the Fourth of July. We drove up to Camelback Mountain and parked overlooking the lights of the city. We talked for a long time.

"I've made a huge mistake," he said. "I've realized how much I still love you, and I want us to be together."

All the words I wanted to hear. *Yippee!* I thought. *I won!* My heart raced, and we laughed and kissed and drove back to my apartment. We celebrated by jumping into bed, and our relationship resumed. I knew we were meant to be together. My fairy tale was back on track, and I knew happily ever after was waiting for me. We were together again, just like we were supposed to be.

However, to my family Steve was the bad boy who had seduced me and then abandoned me. He wasn't very popular around my parents' house. When we started dating again after giving up the baby, my mom was furious. Every time we broke up, I think she did a little victory dance. I also seem to remember that Ronny, my bad-boy older brother, beat the crap out of Steve one night and told him to stay away from me.

One Saturday night in the late winter of 1968, Steve dropped me off from a date around eleven and I decided this was the time to tell my parents that we were going to get married. He was too chicken to come in with me, so I went in the house and told my mom I wanted to talk to her. We sat down in the living room so I could tell her the news that she did not want to hear. I was excited and happy; she was not either of those.

"Mom, you know how much I love Steve, and after all we've been through together, we want to spend the rest of our lives together." I watched my mom's face turn to stone as she just closed up. I rushed on, "We are going to get married. We've figured it all out. We want a small wedding and reception, and we want to get married in just a few weeks." Mom just sat there. "Say something, Mom."

"What do you want me to say? You are too young. You're not right for each other. He makes you cry, and you're always breaking up. Why do you think this will work?"

We took our positions: me trying to convince her that this was right, she trying to get me to grasp what a mistake this was. We had a screaming fight, followed by her storming into her room and slamming the door. I could hear her crying and my dad yelling. Steve had gone back to his parent's house and told me he would wait by the phone to hear how my mom and dad took the news. As soon as my mom went back to her room I called him and sobbed while I told him how terrible my parents were. He said his parents didn't react as strongly; they knew the writing was on the wall.

Sometime after midnight, Mom came into my room with a dry face and sat on the edge of my bed. I thought, *Okay here comes round two.* Instead, she sat down next to me on the bed, took put her arm around me, and said, "Let's start planning this wedding."

"What?" I was shocked. "Why the change of heart?"

"Dee Dee, I know you love Steve, or you think you do. I also know there's nothing I can do to convince you to wait or to change your mind. I was there once too. I was only twenty when I married your dad, and nothing my mother said could convince me otherwise. I wish you would wait until your older, but you won't, and I know you well enough to know that you're going to do this with me or without me. The more I fight you on this, the more you will resent me, and I don't want that to happen. So although I don't agree with it, I will support your decision. Let's plan this wedding. We need to find a place, look for a dress …"

I was dumfounded. I have never forgotten that conversation with my mom.

●　　●　　●

In April of 1968, Steve and I had a small but lovely church wedding with the reception in my parents' back yard. My parents had a beautiful home, and we couldn't afford—nor did we want—a big lavish wedding, so it worked out perfectly.

Our friends and family decorated and cooked and organized and moved furniture, and somehow it all came together. In the late afternoon, we left for the church—that would be a Mormon church, of course. I hadn't been active in the church since I was a young teenager, but my mom wouldn't even consider telling her parents why I wasn't having a Mormon wedding. The guilt rolled downhill, and I wasn't strong enough to stand up for myself or to hurt my grandparents.

The back yard had been decorated with white tablecloths and little bouquets of flowers and twinkling lights floating in the pool. While we were in the church, we were surprised by a classic Arizona thunderstorm, complete with a downpour that drenched everything. If I'd been looking for a sign, I might have paid a little more attention to that. But since I knew I had Prince Charming and my fairy tale was on track, I didn't think of it that way. By the time we got to the house, someone had cleaned up the soggy tablecloths, relit the candles, and refreshed the drenched flowers. We had a wonderful reception.

For our honeymoon Steve and I went up to northern Arizona and stayed in a cabin in the mountains for a few days. When we came home, we moved into a dinky one-bedroom apartment in central Phoenix. He was working at a gas station, and I was working in a small office. I don't know how we made ends meet. We did love each other very much, and I was happy but so insecure. Our relationship had been rocky in the past, and I was so unsure of myself (and to be honest, unsure of him) that I nearly drove him crazy. I was jealous and questioned everything he did when I wasn't with him. If he was late coming home from work, I wanted to know why; if he went out with his buddies, I asked for him details. I really believed if I didn't make the perfect dinners, keep the house perfectly clean, and be the perfect little homemaker, he would leave me. I don't even recognize that person now and have a hard time remembering how to describe her.

Steve was one of the first people who started helping me believe in myself. He believed in me a lot more than I did, but he also got tired of reassuring me constantly and answering my ten thousand questions when he was running ten minutes late. I still had a lot of personal growth ahead of me then, but I'll always remember how much he supported me and tried to get me to see myself as others did. Steve always encouraged me to take a risk and try for a better position at work. He always told me I was the prettiest girl at the party or that I was smart.

I wish I could have believed him.

CHAPTER FOUR

1971 Amy

In 1970, Steve started working as a plumber's apprentice, and I started working at Arizona State University. Our lives and income were stable, and we were happy. In the late fall of 1970, we discovered we were going to have a baby—and this one we could keep!

We were thrilled, and I was so excited I could hardly stand it. In our private moments, it certainly made us mourn the baby we had given up and question our decisions all over again, but we couldn't change that. We could not go backward, and now we had a second chance. Once again, that happily-ever-after thing was heading my way. I hoped that maybe the hole in my heart would finally get filled up.

We couldn't wait to tell our family and friends, and the few people who knew our history were especially excited for us. My mom worked at Goldwater's department store, and I remember the day we walked into the store to tell her our news. We were ecstatic, and she was thrilled for us. By this time, she and Steve had mended all their old wounds and had a good relationship. I beamed as he hugged her and called her "Grandma."

We were still living in our tiny one-bedroom apartment, so we found a bigger apartment right next door to our best friends. We scoured yard sales and second-hand stores for a crib and dresser, which Steve painted. We spent the spring and early summer moving, decorating the baby's room, and doing all the things new parents do, things we could not share before. It was such a great time, anticipating the arrival of this new baby.

I had a good pregnancy, and this time I loved every moment of it. I knew there would be a happier outcome. My due date was July 15, and I woke up that morning with cramps. I wasn't very concerned; I'd been having them off and on for a few days. I had been to the doctor just a few days earlier, and he said we weren't there yet. He also said the baby was breech, meaning it was turned the wrong way—feet first instead of head first—but it would hopefully turn before I delivered.

By nine in the morning, I was getting very uncomfortable and decided I should call the doctor.

"I'm having a lot of low back pain and some mild contractions every once in a while."

"Come on into the office, and I'll check things out. I don't think it's time, but we'll see."

Steve and I arrived at the doctor's about nine thirty that Wednesday morning. After a very short wait, he examined me and leaned back. "You should go home, get your things together, and check into the hospital later this morning. You're in very early labor, but the baby is still feet first in the birth canal," he explained. "I want to see if we can get the baby to turn before you deliver."

"Is everything all right?" I asked, nervous, of course.

"Everything is fine. I'll meet you at the hospital in a few hours. Because your contractions are mild and at irregular intervals, we'll probably have a long labor."

I was uncomfortable but not in serious pain.

I was really getting excited and nervous but trying not to show Steve. He was nervous enough for both of us. When we left the doctor's office, I suggested we stop at the store to get a few things.

"Are you sure you can walk around the store? Should I get you a wheelchair?"

I laughed. "I'm fine. I don't feel any worse than I have felt the last few days. I promise I'll tell you if anything changes." When we got home and put the groceries away, I finished packing my toiletries, and we got ready to go.

As we were driving to the hospital, I started getting a little worried. My pain was getting worse, and the contractions were getting closer together. It was about a twenty-minute drive, and by the time we arrived around eleven o'clock, I was breathing hard. "Now I need that wheelchair."

Steve ran and got the wheelchair, helped me get in, and then rolled me into the lobby of the hospital. Suddenly everything changed. I started having major contractions, and they were coming fast. I was doubled over, crying out each time the pain washed over me. A nurse grabbed my chair and rushed me into a room. She helped me get up on the bed, checked me, and immediately started prepping me for delivery. "I'm going to call the doctor and let him know this will not be a long labor after all."

While she was gone, Steve found my room and paced back

and forth while I writhed in pain. All of a sudden, I felt something very strange between my legs.

"Steve, there's something wrong." I gasped with pain.

He grabbed my hand. "What's wrong? What do you need?"

"I can feel something between my legs. You need to look and see if I'm bleeding or something."

"Really? You want me to look under there?" he hesitantly asked.

"Yes!" I screamed.

"I can't do it." As he very slowly lifted the sheet just enough to look under it, I could see all the color drain from his face. I thought he was going to pass out. "There's a foot coming out!" and then he went running out of the room and into the hall yelling for help.

I called after him. "Steve, come back! Don't leave me alone in here!"

Within moments nurses rushed in, took one look under the sheets, and rushed my bed out the door and down the hall to the birthing room.

As the nurses were getting me situated, the doctor came in rolling up his sleeves. The nurses said: "No time to scrub. The baby's halfway out. Get in there!"

Someone put a mask over my face as I raked my nails down the side of the bed. Everything went dark. As I started waking up, they were showing me a beautiful baby girl. Steve was still out in the hall trying to reach family members on the pay phone as they wheeled me back out to recovery, followed by our baby in her little bed. It was so quick he didn't even realize it was his daughter being whisked past him.

Our beautiful little baby girl was born only forty-five minutes after we got the hospital. We had our baby, and this time no one was taking her away from us. A few hours later, when I held her the first time, all I felt was love and joy. She was tiny, pink, and beautiful. Steve was head over heels, and so was I. The instant I looked at her amazing face, I knew I would walk through fire for this child.

We were supposed to take our baby home on Sunday, and we still hadn't named her. I don't know why it was so difficult; we weren't in disagreement about a name. We just couldn't come up with anything perfect enough for her. The hospital was getting annoyed, because they really needed to complete her birth certificate. We finally decided on the name that expressed what we felt. "Amy" means beloved, and nothing else seemed to fit.

We took her home from the hospital on Sunday morning and tried to figure out what the heck to do with her. We were both very nervous and, like most new parents, didn't really know what we were supposed to be doing. Thank goodness our next-door neighbors and best friends, Mike and Marlene, were already parents. After spending the afternoon getting settled, we knocked on their door and asked them to come meet our daughter. Mike was at work, but Marlene could hardly wait. It was evening and she bent over the bassinet to look at our beautiful Amy. "Dee Dee, she's beautiful, but do you think her coloring is a little bit pale? Come look."

I stepped over to the bassinet and looked in. "Steve, come here. Something's not right. Amy isn't very pink." I picked her up to show Steve.

"I think she looks fine. Maybe it was just the lighting," he said.

I had to agree; she did look pinker than she had when she was lying down. "It's starting to get dark outside, so she must have been in a shadow or something," I said.

So, of course, the three of us anxiously stood over the bassinette just staring at her. As we watched, her color started fading again. She would be pink one minute, and then almost turn blue the next. Was it our imagination? Were we just being paranoid? None of us knew for sure. Luckily, Marlene's husband worked in the emergency room of the local hospital, so we called him and said we were going to bring her in. He told us he would let the doctors know and get us in right away.

We piled in our rickety old pickup and headed for the hospital. They immediately took her to an examining room while we paced in the lobby. I didn't do a lot of pacing as I was still sore, but I was a nervous wreck and could barely contain my fear. After what seemed like an eternity but was probably only about thirty minutes, some doctor brought her out, handed her back to me, and then patted me on the hand. Patted me on the hand!

He gave us a look like we had just wasted his time and said something like: "Now, we know that all new parents are a little anxious at first, but there's nothing wrong with your baby. She's perfectly healthy."

I had also put in a call to my pediatrician—whom I had only met once in the hospital—and naturally got his service, as it was a Sunday night. I don't know whether it was mother's intuition or just nerves, but I just didn't feel comfortable taking her home. I called again from the hospital and told the service that the doctor needed to call us immediately. Just as we were walking out of the hospital, he called and asked me a few questions. He said he would meet us at his office in twenty minutes—at ten o'clock on a Sunday night.

We drove about fifteen minutes to the office, and as we handed Amy to the doctor, she turned blue. He rushed her inside, spent a few minutes checking her, and then called Good Samaritan Hospital to tell them he was bringing her in.

Again we were on our way. We were fortunate that Good Sam was a major hospital close by that had a large neonatal unit. Steve rode with the doctor in his car with an oxygen mask on Amy, and I drove the rickety old truck and followed them to the hospital. It only took about fifteen minutes to get there, but it seemed to take forever. I hurt all over and was so scared I could hardly drive. Was this really supposed to be part of my fairy tale?

Again we waited while they took Amy away from us. As soon as we'd arrived at the hospital, we had started calling immediate family and had a whole contingent of family members roaming the halls within the hour. We were at the hospital until early morning while they examined and ran tests, but they could find nothing wrong with her. No more signs of blue baby; however, they wanted to keep her for observation and to run some additional tests to be sure. I was twenty-three years old with a three-day-old baby, and she was in the neo-natal unit of a hospital. We finally went home about four o'clock in the morning and tried to get a few hours sleep, but it was impossible. This wasn't in my plan. This was not in my fairy tale. This could not be happening. I had to fight my worst fear: *Is this baby going to be taken away from us?*

●   ●   ●

Amy was in the hospital for a week. We spent most of every day there and held her when we could. It was so frightening to see that little tiny thing with tubes and wires all over her. What was even more frightening was to see the other babies who were even smaller and sicker than Amy. Not a very pleasant place to spend your first week as new parents. The doctors and nurses tested and poked at her for a week but could find nothing wrong. She never had another "blue" episode. They sent her home, saying she was fine.

I was a nervous new mother. I watched her constantly to see if she was pink. After days and then weeks with no more signs of trouble, we thought it was just a scare. We settled in to normal new-baby routines: sleepless nights, spit up, and poopy diapers. We spent the next couple of months learning what it was like to be parents of an infant. I was so scared I was going to do something wrong. I kept *The Parenting Handbook* open on her dresser all the time and flipped through the pages every time she made a sound. I looked in it to see if her poop was the right color and consistency. I looked in it if she didn't burp, or if she spit up. We didn't have the internet to look up information and get answers, so I bought more parenting books trying to find out how to be the perfect mom. I was only twenty-three and really had no idea what I was doing. My mom had raised five kids, so I called her often. She was a big help, but none of her kids had started life in such a frightening way. I was so afraid that if I made a mistake, Amy would end up back in the hospital. It was exhausting.

●   ●   ●

In September we took Amy to the pediatrician for her two-month check up. After he examined her, he asked us to come into his office. As we sat across from him, I could see this was not going to be a normal consultation. He was trying to choose his words carefully.

"Amy's head seems to be growing too fast. Now, there are several things that could cause this, but I suspect hydrocephalus."

I wasn't sure I knew exactly what that was, but it was a big ugly word. It flashed in huge, red neon letters in front of my face while I tried to listen to him. Later I looked up the medical definition and learned: "Hydrocephalus is a buildup of excess cerebrospinal fluid within the brain. The excess fluid can increase pressure in the baby's brain, possibly resulting in brain damage and loss of mental and physical abilities." But at that moment, all it meant was my baby was very, very sick.

The doctor wanted her in the hospital that afternoon and told us we should expect surgery within a few days. He called in Dr. John Eisenbeiss, one of the most respected neurosurgeons in the Southwest. We were lucky enough to live near St Joseph's Hospital, with its new Barrow's Neurological Institute. It was also well known for specializing in pediatric neurology.

We drove straight to the hospital from the doctor's office and got Amy settled in her room. Within a couple of hours, Dr. Eisenbeiss came in to see her. He was a tall, very distinguished-looking man with white hair. He was probably in his sixties. He had the bedside manner of Attila the Hun. He didn't introduce himself to Steve or me; he just walked straight over to Amy's bed. He took just a few minutes to examine her and proclaimed, "This baby does not exhibit the typical symptoms of hydrocephalus. She should be lethargic and non-responsive, but she responds to movement and touch. She is animated and active. We'll have to run some tests to see what's going on."

And with that, he left the room. Steve and I looked at each other, having no idea what that meant. Fortunately we had a pediatrician who was kind and warm and easy to talk to. He spent many hours translating, explaining, and guiding us through the medical maze we were entering.

The next morning the doctors started doing tests. For days and days they did tests to that poor little body. They hooked her up to monitors; they stuck her with huge needles all hours of the day; they put tubes in her and dye in her veins; they drew blood; on and on, every day.

Throughout it all Amy seemed to have developed some coping skills. Doctors and nurses were constantly commenting on how happy and bright she was. On days that she didn't have something probing or sticking her, we would find her in various parts of the hospital with one of the nurses. Sometimes they just kept her in the nurse's station in a playpen. The only thing they asked was that we bring her a different blanket from home that allowed air to move through it. She liked to burrow under blanket when she slept. She had her stuffed lion with her at all times. It was her very first gift, given to her several months before she was born by Steve's mom. It was yellow with orange ears, and it played "You Are My Sunshine." She liked to go to sleep listening to it and held it constantly. Amy still has that lion—and it still plays. That, of course, became our song, and when she was little I sang it to her a thousand times.

At the end of September, after two weeks of testing and monitoring, there was still had no conclusive diagnosis. Dr. Eisenbeiss met with several other neurologists, but they could not agree on what exactly was wrong. The only option was exploratory surgery. About ten o'clock one night, Steve and I were leaving the hospital for home in an attempt to get a few hours sleep. As we walked out of her room, Dr. Eisenbeiss was standing in the hallway speaking with another doctor.

Steve asked, "Have you scheduled surgery? Can you please tell us exactly what you'll be doing and what we can expect? Is Amy going to be okay?"

In a language that was supposed to be English but was more neuro-speak, Dr. Eisenbeiss quietly told us that he believed there was a great chance that Amy had a brain tumor, and that they suspected there was little they could do for her.

"We are going to operate on Amy tomorrow morning. We will remove a piece of her skull and see if we can find a tumor. If we find what we suspect, there is at least a 90 percent chance that this tumor is malignant and there won't be anything we can do. We will probably just close her up and let her die peacefully. That's what you should prepare for."

The hall around us closed in on me, and the edges of my vision went dark. My knees got week as I reached for the wall to keep myself from falling.

Prepare? How do you prepare for something like that? Steve and I were both so frightened, trying to make sense of the fact that we might lose this baby. I don't think either of us slept for more than a few minutes that night. We just held on to each other and prayed.

On September 30 we spent all morning holding and loving Amy until they took her away for surgery. Then we paced the bland, beige hospital halls and waited for five very long hours. When the doctor finally came to us in the waiting room he said, "Amy is in recovery. She came through the surgery fine. But I have some good news and some bad news. The good news is it was not a brain tumor as we suspected."

We hardly had time to breathe a sigh of relief before he broke the bad news. "Amy's head was so filled with spinal fluid it caused her brain to be pushed into one side of her head." He demonstrated with his hands that her brain was only occupying about the half the space it should because there was so much fluid not draining out of her brain properly. He explained that they had drained the fluid, and the plan was to let her brain settle back in place and see what happened next. It was hard to understand all of his medical jargon, but we knew she wasn't going to die. I don't know if I heard much more. When they brought her back from recovery, she was a sad little sight with the right side of her head swollen, tubes all over her, and a large horseshoe-shaped incision covered in bandages on the side of her little head.

By the time we took Amy home two weeks after her surgery, she was just over three months old and had spent an entire month in the hospital. But she finally could be home with us, sleeping in her own crib instead of a hospital bed. The future, however, was still unclear. The prognosis: wait and see. It was wonderful to have her home, but also scary. The doctor saw her every week, and we measured her head every day. About two months later, her head started to swell again, so she went back into the hospital.

After a few days of tests, they performed her second surgery on December 1. This time they put two little tubes filled with holes into the lobes of her brain so the fluid could drain out of her head and into her spinal cord. They explained that they were not sure this procedure was going to work, but it was the least invasive procedure, and it had a fairly good chance to be successful. The surgery was performed, and the doctors felt it went well. After a few days of recovery, we took her home again.

After another two months of constant monitoring, her head started swelling again, and back to the hospital we went. This time they did more tests and said her problem seemed to be a rather complicated one with the blockage being at the base of her brain, which is evidently not the norm for hydrocephalus. Oh great! We got to be in the medical journal because of her unusual case. This time they said they would have to install a shunt. Shunts are common today, but in the early 1970s, they had not been around all that long. The surgery involved a little rubber ball implanted in her skull with a tube that ran down into her abdominal cavity for the fluid. They explained we would have to pump the little ball several times every day to make sure the excess fluid was draining from her head.

Her third surgery was January 21, 1972; she was just six months old. Dr. Eisenbeiss told us they were taking a more aggressive approach this time. There could be some consequences, but it was necessary. Again, the surgery seemed to last forever, but this time when he came to us in the waiting room, he said he believed they had been successful.

However, there was still bad news: "To get the shunt in the right place, we had to go cut through a lot of brain tissue. We don't know yet exactly how much damage has been done or how it will show itself. We know the left side of her body will be affected, and it could be extensive. She may never walk or have use of her left arm or leg."

We would just have to wait and see how she developed. He said if she ever takes those first steps, we'd know she could walk. Until then, there was really no way to know. Not exactly great news, but at least she was alive.

When they brought her out of recovery, we saw the gurney being wheeled down the hall. Amy was awake and alert. She was sitting up in bed holding her lion. The doctors and nurses were amazed. She had this incredible resiliency and spirit that was not to be explained. I don't know the answer to the nature versus nurture argument, but this little girl came into the world with strength and fight and stamina. We would come to know that this tough little girl would continue surprising doctors and family for years to come.

There was more news. Dr. Crawford, her pediatrician, came to see us after his hospital rounds, as he did most nights. He was so helpful in answering our questions and explaining these very complicated procedures to us. He sat down and walked us through the next phase of her recovery. "You need to understand that there will need to be more surgeries to lengthen the tube as her body grows. She's only about thirty inches long now, and the tube running from her brain to her abdominal cavity is coiled to allow room for growth. But it will have to be extended. I think you should expect at least two to three more surgeries until her body stops growing."

Steve and I could only nod.

"Also, shunts are not perfect," he continued. "They clog easily, and it's common to have to replace them periodically."

At that time, a two-year-old boy in the bed next to Amy in her hospital room was in for his fourteenth shunt revision because of complications. If Amy got a bacterial infection and a fever, or at any time she acted lethargic, we were to watch for signs of brain swelling. We were not out of the woods by any means.

It was so hard to see my beautiful little baby with her head so swollen, tubes everywhere, machines hooked to every part of her body. But she smiled and laughed. I never took any pictures of Amy in the hospital because I didn't think I would ever be able to look at them. Today I wish I had some photos to show her the history of her early life. But I will forever have those images of her burned in my memory.

The nurses and doctors at the hospital loved Amy's spirit and had all practically become family, as we had been there for a good part of her first six months. This time when she came home, the doctors said, "We'll know when we know."

●　　　●　　　●

So life started to get back to normal—not that we knew exactly what that was. Amy was approaching seven months old, and we didn't even know what normal looked like. I was afraid to let her out of my sight. If she spit up, if she sneezed, if she didn't eat, I would worry. I would walk into her room several times during the night to see if she was breathing. I was constantly afraid and extremely overprotective.

The one complication that would send me reeling was her seizures. She started having them a few months after her final surgery. She would just stop breathing periodically, turn a little blue, and then start breathing again. Nothing to it! The first time it happened, I frantically called my pediatrician, ready to run to the emergency room. He quickly calmed me down and said seizures were not unusual; they were known as abortive seizures, meaning they would stop on their own and they would not kill her. The doctors said I did not need to panic and rush her into the hospital every time she had one. Just stay calm.

Easy for them to say. The doctor put her on medication to help control the seizures, but they didn't go away completely As she got a little older, she had some way of knowing they were coming. She would stop whatever she was doing, walk over to me, look right at me, and then just stop breathing for a moment. She could sense that one was coming on soon and get very still. It would last twenty or thirty seconds, and then it would end. Her color would turn good again, and she would just go back to whatever she had been doing. There didn't seem to be an after-effect of any kind for her. Me? I would just about go into cardiac arrest as she would turn around to go on her merry way. It took her about five seconds to recover, but it usually took me thirty minutes or so to start breathing normally again. She continued to have seizures until she was five years old, when they just gradually went away.

Thankfully, Amy was a happy, easygoing baby. She was content just looking at the ceiling for hours, and if a toy was out of reach, oh well. Of course, everything she *didn't* do scared us. Should she be crawling by now? Is it bad that she's not trying harder to do things? I called my pediatrician more times than I'd like to admit. Every time I called, they were patient and understanding. They must have been tired of hearing it was me on the phone, but they never let me know that. We had such great doctors and nurses every step of the way with Amy.

As the days and weeks went by, we anxiously watched her every move. When she was nine or ten months old, we spent way too much time trying to get her to crawl. But she didn't think she'd do that, not for a toy, not for a snack. It was just more effort that she wanted to put out. Instead, she rolled everywhere she wanted to go and spent hours rolling over and over down the hallway to get from one room to the other. One more thing to add to my worry list: did this mean she wouldn't be able to walk?

●　　　●　　　●

On her first birthday, we had family and close friends over to our little apartment for a birthday party and a celebration of our miracle. She was happy and healthy and, up to this point, developing as she should. She had enough hair that you could barely see the scars on the side of her head, and her shunt was functioning properly with no mishaps or scares. I sat on the floor while Amy rolled around to get from person to person. Every parent wants their baby to walk, but with that comes the natural expectation that when the time is right, they will get up and take their first steps. We had no way to know if that day would ever come. We had been working with her, trying to get her to take some steps for weeks, but she just wasn't ready. Every day she didn't take that first step, it worried me. She was able to pull herself up and stand, but that was it. I know many babies don't walk by their first birthday, but I wanted so badly to know that she could.

Evidently she decided she liked being the center of attention that day, because about halfway through the birthday party, as she was holding on to the coffee table, she turned and took two steps and then sat down. Everyone in the room immediately got quiet. I think we were afraid to breathe, so we just watched her. A few minutes later, as we all sat staring at her, she got up again and took about ten steps across the room for the first time.

You would have thought she just walked on the moon. We yelled and screamed—I cried—and everyone cheered so loudly we practically scared her to death. A little while later, after the hysteria died down, she did it again and then again. Today, I can still see her holding her arms out wide with a great big smile on her face as she walked up to me. *Oh my God. She can walk!*

After that, Amy seemed to progress at what seemed to be a normal pace. I finally figured out that she was just content and easy-going. As she grew, most of her motor skills developed adequately but slowly. Her nickname was Squirt because she smaller than most of the kids her age. She couldn't run as fast or jump as high, but no one knew that she had any health issues of any kind.

The biggest obstacle in her world was that by the time she was six, she still couldn't skip. Her feet just wouldn't do it like the other kids. It was a very big deal to her. As she approached her sixth birthday, learning to skip was practically an obsession. It was going to be the greatest achievement of her life. When the doctors had told us after that last surgery that they didn't know whether she would ever walk, the other possibility was that she may not have use of the left side of her body, or possibly very limited use. We knew the left side of her body worked, but something just wasn't quite right with her left leg. You couldn't tell by looking at her, but it just didn't always work like it was supposed to.

Amy didn't know why she couldn't skip, but she knew other little girls her age could. She worked so hard at it and, at the recommendation of her doctors, took ballet and gymnastics to help her develop good motor function. After several weeks of ballet classes, she had her first dance recital. She practiced and practiced in her room but would never let me watch. On the day of the big performance, she was very excited to perform "The Dance of the Scarves." She looked adorable in her pink leotard and frilly tutu, her long, thick, honey-colored hair tied back with pink ribbons.

When it was time to start, I handed her the bright purple-and-blue scarves from my purse and got down on my knees to give her a hug and little pep talk. "Amy, I know you're going to be great! You just do you very best, and it's ok if you don't skip."

"Don't worry, Mommy. I can do it."

I stood up with tears in my eyes, and she ran and took her place as the last in line. There's nothing cuter than a bunch of six-year-old little girls who truly believe they are ballerinas. They beamed as they danced, and Amy did a good job of keeping up with them. As we came closer to the end of the performance, my heart was in my throat as I watched the other little girls, because I knew Amy could not skip like they did.

When it came her turn, I gave her a big supportive smile from across the room, and she gave me a great big smile back. Then I watched her skip across the room, waving her scarves up and down, while tears streamed down my face. She was so proud of herself. The teacher, who knew a little of her medical history, stood next to me and cried with me. It was an Olympic gold medal achievement. The other mothers must have thought I was a little crazy to be so emotional at a six-year-old's dance recital, but they would never know how important it was to see Amy's accomplishment. It was a very big deal.

Soon after that, we had an appointment with the neurosurgeon, and she wanted to surprise him as well. Neurosurgeons are not generally known for their bedside manner, and Dr. Eisenbeiss was no exception. Most of the time he was all business. But Amy was special to him. He was kind and gentle with her, and I know he had a soft spot for his amazing little patient. He put her through the standard battery of tests: he checked her reflexes, had her walk across the room, hop on one foot, and several other things to check her coordination and motor skills.

When he finished his exam, he told me how pleased he was with her progress. He said her motor functions were coming along nicely.

Amy interrupted him. "Dr. Eisenbeiss, I have a surprise."

"Oh really? What might that be?"

"I'll show you, but you have to move out of the way." Then she asked me for her scarves and walked to the far side of the room. She let out a little giggle and started humming the music from her recital as she skipped all around his office waving her scarves.

He had the biggest smile on his face. He told me that day, after practicing medicine for nearly forty years, Amy was his first miracle. He had no explanation for her progress and lack of complications, but he would not question it. He just said he had always hoped for a miracle. That was the only explanation he had.

The seizures were gone, she was running, jumping, and skipping like every other child, and he had no idea why except the incredible power of the human spirit. How could one not go through life with hope when you lived with a miracle? Every day for nearly forty years, I have given thanks for her. She has blessed my life in so many ways and given me reason to go on in my very darkest moments. What I didn't know then was how she would pull me through even rougher times ahead.

●　　●　　●

Amy was my miracle, but she was also an independent, self-sufficient little stinker at times. One day when she was six years old, I took her to her gymnastics class. I would usually drop her off on Saturday mornings and pick her up two hours later. On this particular day, I decided to run errands to pass the time. I went to the nearest mall and made good use of my free time. A while later, I checked my watch and saw that I still had plenty of time to kill, so I went on to do a few more things. When I got back in the car, the clock had a very different time than my watch did. My watch had stopped, and I was nearly thirty minutes late picking Amy up.

I sped to the gymnastics building and there was Amy, standing all alone in front.

Oh my gosh, poor little thing. She must be scared to death, crying her eyes out. But wait. She has her arms crossed, and she's tapping her foot on the sidewalk.

"Where have you been?" she yelled. "Do you know how late you are?"

I bent down, put my arms around her, and told her how sorry I was. I then looked at her and said, "I thought you'd be crying and scared, but you're not. What were you going to do if I didn't show up?"

"I was just getting ready to call a taxi," she stated.

"Really? And how were you going to pay for this taxi?"

She said, "I would have figured that out once I got home."

I didn't bother to ask her if she knew our address.

●   ●   ●

About this same time, she decided we should be on a first-name basis. We were driving down the street one day, and she asked me if we could stop for ice cream. Instead of calling me Mommy she said, "Dee Dee, can we stop for ice cream?"

Huh! That's odd, I thought. "So what happened to 'Mommy'? Why are you calling me by my name?"

She said, "Well, you don't call me Daughter do you? You always say my name, so I will too."

Well, that's interesting and kind of logical, I guess. It only lasted about a week, but I thought it was a fascinating peek into the way her brain worked.

●   ●   ●

Then there are those moments when your child teaches you one of life's lessons. When Amy was seven, she was on the girls' softball team. She was the smallest on the team and without doubt the worst player. She would get out there every game and never hit or catch the ball, but she didn't care. One time, after a particularly bad performance, I talked to her as we were walking off the field. "You know, Amy, you could play on the younger team with the smaller girls. Maybe you'd get to play more."

She looked at me like I had two heads and said, "Mom, just because I'm not the best doesn't mean I shouldn't play. I'm staying on this team."

For a good part of my life, I believed I wasn't good enough, and it kept me from trying new things, from taking chances because I was afraid to fail. As I've gotten older, I've worked hard to build my self-confidence, to learn to believe in myself and to trust my intuition. Too bad I didn't have her attitude sooner.

The girls on the team kind of adopted her as their mascot. Instead of teasing and bullying her because she played so badly, they rallied around her and supported her. During the last game of the season, when she went up to bat, she finally hit the ball. It only went about three feet, but she hit it! Her teammates came off the bench and carried her around the field to home plate. She laughed and giggled all the way.

●   ●   ●

When Amy was eight, we went to see Dr. Eisenbeiss, her neurologist, who gave us the sad news that he was retiring but wanted to see Amy one last time. He hadn't seen her in two years because she hadn't had any of the problems that were anticipated. He put Amy through all the standard tests and once again pronounced her to be his only miracle. She really was in the medical journals; there had never been a case of a shunt that had not been replaced in eight years for either growth or malfunction.

As we sat and talked about all Amy had been through and Dr. Eisenbeiss talked about his hope for her future, he said, "You know, my educated guess is that for some reason she doesn't need the shunt anymore. I really don't believe it's doing anything; shunts are just not this problem-free." He looked at her carefully. "My curiosity really wants to know, but they only way to find out is to go in and remove it."

I gasped. "You mean surgery? Just to satisfy your curiosity? I don't think so."

He chuckled. "I know, I know. It's not worth the risk. If she is passing just one drop a day through the shunt, she needs it, and I would never take that kind of chance. But I sure am curious."

"Well, I suppose I am too, but not enough to put her in the hospital. We'll just have to wonder."

That was the last time we saw Dr. Eisenbeiss. It was hard to say good-bye to this man who had saved my child's life. She did not see another neurosurgeon until she was seventeen.

●   ●   ●

Amy continued to do well and showed no signs of physical problems. Every time she had a cold or a fever, I went into a tailspin and watched her like a hawk, but she always came out of it without a problem. When she was in fourth grade, her teacher thought she should be tested for learning disabilities. School had been a struggle for her every year, and it wasn't getting any better.

She was put through a battery of tests, and the psychologists were quite surprised to discover that she had some serious learning disabilities in a couple of areas, but because she had developed such good compensation skills on her own, they had gone undiscovered for several years.

Amy was very nervous and upset about going through the tests. She had a hard time testing, and they had to repeated some of them a few times. She would just freeze up.

When they were finally complete, she was pretty darn happy to find out she had learning disabilities. When we sat down with the psychologist to learn about the results of her tests, Amy had a reaction I was not prepared for. As it was being explained to her, I could see her eyes get red and start to tear up.

I said, "Amy, it's okay, this is good news. We're finding out how to help you learn better."

"No, Mom, I'm not sad. I'm happy. I thought I was stupid, and now I know I'm not."

"No, Amy," I said, "you are most definitely not stupid."

Every day she had to leave her regular classroom for a couple of hours to go to her special ed classes. She was embarrassed about it at first, so she made up a different excuse each day for where she was going. One day she said, "Mom, you know I thought I was stupid, but every day I tell Sarah I'm going to the dentist or the doctor or somewhere, and she's been believing me for months. Maybe I'm not the stupid one."

Comprehension and retention were the two areas that showed the strongest degree of disability, but she learned new skills to help her. She never gave up. With the help of her special education classes, Amy improved in school, but it was never easy. High school was always a challenge, but she maintained a good grade-point average and excelled on the swim team. Her high school graduation was one special night for all of us.

•   •   •

Shortly after Amy finished high school, when she was seventeen, we had another scare. Her dad called me to say she wasn't feeling well. (She had been living with him for a couple of years; more about that drama later.) He told me she was lethargic and the tube from her shunt was swollen. I thought, *Well, this is it. The other shoe has finally dropped.* We had to find a new neurosurgeon and get all of her records together and then explain her entire medical history to this stranger who sat there with his mouth gaping open as we finished her story.

This doctor looked at me and said in utter amazement, "You mean to tell me that this girl with this medical history has completed high school, is going to college, and has a job?" I was trying to signal him with my eyes to back off, but he didn't get it.

Amy looked at me and said, "Why is he so surprised? Does he think I shouldn't be doing any of these things?"

Steve and I explained to her and the doctor that we never let her know her limitations. She didn't know she had never been expected to accomplish so much. If we had told her she wasn't supposed to be able to do something, she would have had an easy out, an excuse. She was mad. She thought she had been cheated because we hadn't explained all this to her earlier. I thought she'd been given a chance to be normal and succeed. Thankfully, that episode turned out to be just a scare, and she was fine a couple of days later, once again beating the odds.

To this day Amy has never been back in the hospital for

any problems related to her shunt. She has never had her shunt removed, and she has never had complications that required medical treatment. She has had some close calls, but never another shunt-related surgery.

If you look closely, you can see that her left leg is smaller than her right. Her left foot is almost two sizes smaller than her right, and it turns up a little bit, so she really has problems with shoes. But visibly there are no other signs of her illness.

We'd gone through a lot of turmoil already, Steve and I: the pregnancy, the adoption, Amy's medical issues. But I was still optimistic about life and felt like we were moving forward.

Little did I know that life as we knew was to come to a complete—and awful—halt.

CHAPTER FIVE

1974 Bethany

In the fall of 1973, my sister, Shelley, announced that she and Bob were getting married. Talk about your fairy tale: they had been together since he was the high school football star and she was the blond cheerleader. My sister was like the girl in *American Graffiti*, with beautiful blond hair down to the middle of her back and gorgeous face, and she drove a yellow T-Bird. Perfect fairy-tale stuff. She wanted me to be in the wedding and wanted Amy, who would turn three a month before the wedding, to be the flower girl.

A few months later, as we were making preparations for the August wedding, I found out I was pregnant again, with a due date in August. My mom was a great seamstress, so she decided to make all the bridesmaids dresses, and mine could be custom made to fit. When we realized how close my due date was to the wedding, we all prayed as my mom kept letting out my dress. I was a lovely vision at nearly two hundred pounds with feet so swollen I had to buy slippers to wear for the ceremony. I also had ridiculously short choppy hair that might have looked good on a ninety-pound pixie. I look at those pictures now and just cringe. I was a great big blob of flowing yellow.

To make matters worse, I walked down the aisle with Bob's best friend, a very handsome six-foot-two guy with long blond hair and the face of a model. Poor guy, I bet he would have paid money to get out of that assignment. I somehow managed to waddle through the wedding without wrecking the celebration.

Two weeks later, on August 24, Amy's sister, Bethany, was born. After all we had been through with Amy, I couldn't imagine how I could love this second child as much as I loved Amy. I was not excited about her birth. In addition, I had a difficult pregnancy. I was sick a lot, and the baby pushed on my sciatic nerve for most of the nine months so I had constant pain. Did I mention I was the size of a linebacker?

Steve was excited about this new baby. There were cracks starting to appear in the walls of our marriage, but everyone knows a new baby will make a rocky marriage better. Ha! I wanted to be excited about this baby, and I wanted our marriage to get back on more solid ground. I'm not quite sure how we started drifting apart, but it was obvious we had. When you fall in love as young as we did, there is still so much change and growth in front of you. We just started wanting different things, and we changed separately, not together. How do you ever explain how a marriage starts falling apart?

This pregnancy was difficult from the very beginning. I had a lot of morning sickness, and I was always uncomfortable. During delivery, we found out that I have a tipped uterus. I was advised that any future pregnancies would be even more difficult, and I would probably have difficulty carrying to term. I decided to have my tubes tied right after the delivery. It seemed like the right thing to do at the time, but it was a decision I came to regret.

When Beth finally arrived, Steve was excited to have another girl, but those maternal instincts just didn't kick into high gear for me like they were supposed to. I didn't seem to have the same attachment I had for Amy, and I was filled with guilt. I think I was going through postpartum depression, but we didn't have a name for it then. I did all the things I was supposed to do, but that close bond was not coming easily.

My apathy lasted a couple of months, but then as Bethany's personality started to emerge, so did my love for her. What a little imp. Where Amy had been easy, sweet, and mellow, Beth was anything but. You could just see the mischief dancing in her dark-chocolate eyes. Beth wasn't the prettiest baby (because, of course, Amy was the prettiest baby who had ever been born), but she made up for that with tons of personality—most of it a challenge. Beth was a handful from the beginning; she definitely had a mind of her own. As she grew from an infant into a curious baby, she was into everything. She was determined, willful, and obstinate. She was also funny and precocious, and most importantly she was healthy.

Amy became an instant mother at the age of three and adored Beth from the first moment she saw her. Instead of sibling rivalry and jealousy, Amy announced to everyone that this was her baby. She would let me take care of her sister on occasion, but we needed to know who Beth belonged to. She was Amy's living doll, and Amy doted on her constantly. She wanted to hold her, to feed her, and to change her. As they grew older, they did everything together. I vividly remember Amy making sure Beth was the center of attention when it was time to show off any new talents.

"Look how she can crawl!"

"Watch her walk!"

"She has a new dance to show you," Amy would exclaim.

Beth was funny, and smart, and temperamental. She ran me ragged. She would have things her way—or else. When she was two years old and almost potty trained, she would occasionally have an accident and hide her underwear in the backyard under the bushes. One day when the weather was warm, the girls were out in the backyard playing. As it neared lunchtime, I poked my head out the back door and called to them. Amy came in first and said, "Uh Mommy, Beth lost something."

"What do you mean? What did she lose?" I asked.

Amy ran down the hall laughing. "I'm not telling. You better ask her."

"Beth, Amy said you lost something. What did you lose?"

She lifted up her dress and said, "My underwear!"

Not sure whether to be mad or laugh, I said, "Just where did you lose them?"

"Under the bushes," she replied.

"Bethany Ann, did you wet your pants?"

"Yes Mommy, and I put them under the bushes to dry."

In exasperation, I said, "Beth, you know better! Why did you wet your pants?"

In true Beth fashion, she crossed her arms, looked up at me, and exclaimed, "Because I wanted to!"

That's the way it was to be. Beth had a mind of her own, and she had an answer for everything. She was willful, determined, smart, and precocious. She also loved to sing and had an amazing memory. She could sing along with almost every song she heard on the radio and would remember the words.

•   •   •

Just before Beth's second birthday, Steve got a good business opportunity to work with his brother in northern California. It was a big decision to move away from both of our families, but the job was too good to pass up. We also thought this change might be able to heal some of the bumpy spots that had developed in our marriage. Steve and I were in trouble; my fairy tale was falling apart, and it would not be healed. The problems were getting bigger every day.

We found a small house to rent at first and got settled. Within a few months of our arrival, Steve's brother was promoted and he moved out of state, so we bought his family's home. It was a gorgeous white stucco home in an upscale neighborhood, with a beautiful pool in our back yard. Steve was doing well, the girls were thriving, and I found another job at a radio station working for a woman who would change my life.

I had worked at a radio station in Phoenix before Beth was born, and I really liked it. I had some good references, so I was fortunate to land a similar job in California. I was a receptionist and did some administrative work for the general manager. This station was unique: it was run by a woman, with a female-only sales team, and even a female morning disc jockey. In the seventies that was unheard of.

Working with a lot of women was a wonderful experience. On the other hand, there were many mornings I just felt like putting out a saucer of milk and a scratching post and getting out of everyone's way. Depending on everyone's mood, it could get a little catty every once in a while. However, I learned a lot from these dynamic women while I watched them in action. I thought there were all so much smarter and better than me. I was fortunate that my boss, Judy, saw something different.

Just about every time she walked by my desk, she would say: "You're so much more than this. You have so much to offer." She said it so often it finally started sinking in and making sense.

At home, Steve and I fought all the time. We had different ideas about the kind of lifestyle we each wanted. I wanted him to change and be something he wasn't, and he wanted me to change and get on board with his game plan. Our marriage was in serious trouble. After months and months of trying to find a way to work things out, I just didn't see how we could ever be happy again. I was miserable. After many fights and tears and drama, I made the decision to leave him and take the girls back to Phoenix where I had family support to help me be a single mom.

If I were older and wiser, would I have dealt with our troubles differently? Most likely, but I'll never know. Hindsight is a beautiful thing, and I think, had I known then what I know now, I may have made other choices. One thing I know for sure: if I had to do it over, I would never have taken the girls away from their father, no matter what the circumstances. With what was to come, it's a decision I'll regret for the rest of my days. We can't see the forest for the trees sometimes, and at that time, when I was still not strong enough to believe in myself, I thought I needed to go home.

So in 1977, Steve and I split up. He'd been the love of my life since high school, the guy who was supposed to build my white picket fence for us. We'd been together for twelve years and had been through some incredibly difficult times, yet we couldn't go on the way we were. Right after one of our major fights, where we screamed and yelled at each other, I called my old boss from the radio station where I had worked in Phoenix and told him I was coming back.

"There's a job waiting," he told me, which was reassuring. But at the last minute I backed out. I just couldn't walk out on my marriage without one more try. Actually it turned out to be several more tries. We'd fight, I'd decide I was leaving, call my boss and ask for my job back, and then chicken out. And the pattern would repeat. Fight, decide to leave, back out. Each time, I vowed to try to make the marriage work one more time.

My old boss in Phoenix got really tired of my ever-changing mind and finally said, "Why don't you just call me when you get to town, and we'll see what we can do." Couldn't blame him.

Finally, in July of 1977, I decided there was no other way. We spent Amy's sixth birthday at a theme park, and the next day I packed my little trailer and left northern California to head back to Phoenix. I had such guilt for ending my marriage that I took very little from the beautiful house we lived in: the girl's beds, their clothes and toys, and my clothes. Everything else in the house was left as my guilt sacrifice.

We attached a trailer to my old Audi, made beds in the back seat of the car for the girls (no seat belts in the seventies), and early in the morning in the middle of July, the girls and I started on our journey. I was twenty-nine years old, Amy had just turned six, and Beth was almost three.

The car didn't have the power to pull the trailer and use the air conditioning, so we were hot and uncomfortable. Going up the hills in central California, we had so little power I thought we were going to start rolling backward. I had to be careful where I stopped because I had no idea how to back up a car with a trailer attached. We got to LA during evening rush hour, which added a couple of hours to our trip. As we got to the other side of the city, I was exhausted and thought we should look for a place to spend the night. We had been on the road for over eight hours at this point and were only halfway home. The girls wouldn't have it and wanted to push on, so we did—through the California/Arizona desert at 115 degrees with no air conditioning.

We stopped everywhere we could and got cups of ice. The girls would hold ice cubes on my neck and rub them all over their bodies to keep cool. We looked like three little mud pies. It was absolutely miserable, but I can't remember ever having to scold or get after the girls for anything. They were amazing. We pulled in to Phoenix and headed for my sister's house at midnight, seventeen very long, hot, dusty hours after we had departed. To this day I have no idea how we did it.

● ● ●

The next day I called my old boss at the radio station and told him I was finally in town. He asked me what day I wanted to start work. *Thank you, Gary.* The girls and I had to find housing and daycare, and then I would start working and rebuilding a life for us. I found a cheap apartment and set up house. We had two beds for the girls, and my mother-in-law gave us the rest of our furniture: a rollaway for me, two plastic lawn chairs, a metal TV tray, and a small black-and-white television. We bought some used pots and pans, dishes, and a few basics, and that was it. My brother-in-law's good friend Cheryl ran a daycare center not far away. She fell in love with the girls.

Although our apartment was small and the furnishings were meager, it was my new life, and for the sake of Amy and Beth, I needed to make it work. The girls liked it because there was a big yard where they could play, a pool for the hot evenings after work, and lots of other children around. There were also tons of crickets. When we got home at the end of the day, crickets were everywhere. Amy decided to make them her pets and gave them names. We spent the next few weeks getting settled and into a routine. Who knew my life would come crashing down around me so soon?

Bethany's third birthday was Wednesday, August 24. We had a family birthday party in our apartment with my brother and his wife, my sister, and Steve's mom and sister. My mom and dad were traveling in their motor home and couldn't be there. Bethany got everything she wanted: a new pillow, a tool belt, and cowboy boots. Beth wasn't a real girly girl; she preferred tool belts and boots to dolls and lace. My little three-year-old could not be bothered with dolls when there were things to build and imaginary horses to ride.

I was grateful that my brother took pictures, because I didn't have a camera. Unfortunately those pictures didn't turn out. We never got to see them.

Two days later, on Friday afternoon, just five weeks after we had arrived back in Phoenix and two weeks after I had returned to work, Cheryl called from daycare and said Beth seemed to be coming down with the flu. She had a low fever and was vomiting. I left work about three o'clock and drove thirty minutes to get the girls. When I got to daycare, Beth was curled up on her towel, and Amy was sitting next to her, rubbing her head. It was obvious Beth didn't feel well. Cheryl said she had vomited a couple of times and just wanted to lie down. I took the girls home, and Beth was doing just what kids with the flu did: whining, vomiting, and just obviously not feeling very good. About four thirty, I called our pediatrician, the same one who had taken such good care of Amy, and when he heard it was me, he came right on the line.

"I understand Bethany's not feeling well?" he asked.

"She's vomited a few times and has a fever. Since it's Friday night, I'm afraid to go through the weekend. Could you possibly see her this evening?

He said, "Of course. The flu is going around. That's probably what it is, but let's definitely check her out this evening." With Amy's history, he knew that sick little girls made me extremely nervous.

I packed up the girls and drove through busy evening traffic and got to his office just before six o'clock. He gave her a thorough exam and then said yes, it looked like the flu, and a pretty good case of it at that. Her temperature was not dangerously high but high enough. He checked her motor function, especially her neck, and he assured me it was just routine, checking for signs of meningitis among other things. He said that she would probably be sick most of the night. If it would make me feel better, he offered to hospitalize her so she could get fluids and I wouldn't sit up all night in a panic. (Memories of Amy's illness were still too fresh for me to be very calm.)

I remember him saying specifically that he didn't think she needed to be in a hospital, but he would certainly understand if I felt she would be safer there. I said no, if he didn't think it was absolutely necessary, I was sure we'd be fine. He told me to keep fluids in her and call in the morning to let him know how she was doing. I had no sense of danger. I will always wonder if things would have been different had I made another decision.

We went back to the apartment and got settled. Beth seemed to be feeling a little better. She didn't have an appetite and wanted to go to bed. I checked on her a couple of times during the night, and she was sleeping peacefully. When I woke up in the morning and realized she had slept all night, I was relieved. We had planned to continue her birthday with a trip to the zoo with some friends—maybe we'd get to go after all. I can still see her walking into my room about seven o'clock the next morning, saying, "Mommy, I feel better."

It was early, so I thought I'd give it a little while before I called the doctor and let him know we were doing fine. She curled up on the couch to watch cartoons and soon fell back asleep. I let her rest there for thirty minutes and then started to wake her so I could check on her again before I called the doctor. She wouldn't wake up. She was really sleeping hard.

I picked her up from the couch and put her in my lap and started calling her name.

Amy was sitting next to me. "Beth," she said, "time to wake up! We're going to the zoo." Beth fluttered her eyelids a little but didn't wake up. Amy kept calling to her and then looked at me. "Mommy, why won't she talk to me?"

"I don't know, Amy. I think she's just really tired." But I was starting to get worried.

A moment later Bethany opened her eyes and looked up at me. Then she looked at Amy and smiled.

Amy said, "Come on, Beth, let's get dressed. We're going to the zoo today for your birthday!"

But it was obvious there had been a big change. Beth kept falling asleep and then waking up again, but she wouldn't stay awake very long, she wouldn't answer me when I talked to her, and her skin was blotchy. We probably only sat with her on the couch for ten minutes, but in my memory it went on forever.

She finally woke up and became more alert, but she was weak and didn't want to stand up. She didn't have a fever, but she was obviously not feeling better. I called the doctor and described her symptoms.

He asked me a couple of questions and then said, "I want you to bring her to the office right now. I'll be waiting for you."

On the way to his office, Amy held Beth and said, "Mom, she's breathing funny, and she won't talk to me."

Why didn't I turn and head for a hospital? Because you never think that anything that bad will happen to your children. Even after what Amy had been through, I didn't think this was going to be serious. We just had to get to the doctor's office, and everything would be okay. Why didn't he tell me to go to the emergency room? Why didn't I just go straight to the hospital? I was concerned, but I wasn't scared. Kids get sick; she was just sick.

Her condition had changed fairly drastically on the drive. When the doctor met us at the door, he immediately handed her to a nurse, told her to get in his car, and barked at someone else to call the hospital and tell them to have the trauma unit ready. He got a portable oxygen tank from the office and hooked Beth up while the nurse held her in the passenger seat of his car. Then he jumped in and started the engine.

He yelled, "There's no time to wait for an ambulance. We're going to St. Joe's. You follow us and find us when you get there."

I threw Amy into my car and we followed him.

Amy kept asking questions, of course. "Mommy, what's wrong with Beth? Where are we going?" She had a million questions, and I had no answers.

I finally yelled at her in frustration. "Amy, I don't know. Stop asking!"

She sat there with tears streaming down her face. I felt terrible and told her I was sorry, but I could only concentrate on getting to the hospital as fast as we could.

As we drove up to St. Joseph's hospital, the doctor was just pulling up to a doctor's entrance on the side of the building. He jumped out of his car, grabbed Beth from the nurse, and ran through the door with her.

By the time we parked and found our way to where the doctor had taken Beth, he had handed her off to the specialists who had been called: a cardiologist, an internist, and three other doctors of some kind. Amy and I found our way to a little waiting room and sat down. My eyes focused on the bland beige linoleum on the floor and the tan vinyl couch in the little alcove. *Back in a hospital. Again!* I thought. My brain could hardly absorb the information, and my fear kept me from processing anything normally.

After a few minutes, the pediatrician came out and tried to explain Beth's symptoms. "Beth has a very high fever again and is having trouble breathing. Her system has gone into shock. We're not sure what's wrong, but she has specialist with her, and we're doing everything we can to find the answers."

"Is she going to be okay? What's causing this?"

"There are a lot of people working on her right now; she's very sick. I don't know any more than that yet, but I'll come back out as soon as I know more."

I thought, *Oh no, another hospital stay for one of my children.* That was upsetting, but I would get through it. I had before. This couldn't possibly be any worse than what we'd gone through with Amy. She would be fine. The doctor suggested I make some phone calls to see if I could get some family members to come join me. *Oh boy, this is going to be a long day.*

I don't think I was being ignorant; I was protecting myself. Your brain will just not let you go beyond a certain point. It doesn't know how to process the possibility that your child may die. Even as close as we had come to losing Amy, she had made it. Beth would too. This was not brain trauma; this was just the flu.

There was a pay phone on the wall of the waiting room. I made some phone calls but could not reach anyone: my mom, my sister, Steve's family—all out and about on this Saturday morning. A few minutes passed. The doctor came out and said, "Dee Dee, I'm sorry, but Beth is not doing well."

I took a deep breath. "What does that mean?"

"She's okay right now, but her heart did stop once. They quickly revived it, but she's struggling."

I blurted, "Why did her heart stop? What's wrong with her? Isn't this just the flu? She's going to be all right, isn't she?"

"I hope so, but I don't know. I really want you to get somebody here for support. You shouldn't be going through this alone. If her heart stops again, she could be in trouble."

Wow, this is bad. Now I am really scared, but she'll be okay. It might be a long haul, but she'll be fine.

I told myself, *Look what Amy has survived.* She was my proof that we'd get through this. Beth had never been sick a day in her life, which, as we came to find out, was a very bad thing.

Within just a few minutes, a nurse came up to me and said, "Ma'am, we have a private waiting room just around the corner. I think you and your daughter would be much more comfortable in there. There's a phone you can use more privately."

That's when panic started to set in. *Oh no, I don't want to go to a private waiting room. That could only mean this is really, really serious.* The first real warning signs started going off in my brain, but I had to push them aside in order to function. I reluctantly went to the private room, where a nun came to ask if she could take Amy down to the playroom to keep her occupied. A little while later, maybe ten minutes or so, my pediatrician came back in and said things were not good. He told me we were in danger of losing Beth and I needed someone with me.

Okay, in danger of losing her is bad, but of course, it won't happen.

By this time I was getting very shaky and was calling anyone I could think of. Where was everybody? I finally got through to my sister and told her to try to reach Steve's mom, and to please come to the hospital herself. I needed someone there with me. Somewhere in the confusion of people calling each other, the message got mangled. Everyone who came to the hospital thought it was Amy back in the hospital because of some complication.

I sat in this empty room by myself, waiting and praying. I hadn't been able to see Beth since we'd arrived, and I wanted to see her. After another thirty minutes, one of the doctors walked into the room, and there was a priest with him. I remember looking up at them and just saying, "Oh my God," over and over again. *Why is that other man here? There must be some mistake.*

The doctor came over to me and took my hand. He said, "I am so, so sorry." He didn't say any more than that; he didn't have to. The look on his face told me everything.

I looked at him in disbelief. The priest was standing in front of me, and before I could ask any questions, he said that Beth was with God, in a better place, she was at peace—words that meant nothing to me. *Do not talk to me about a God that just took my daughter away from me!* I sat there trying to take in enough air to breathe without passing out. This could not be real. I was hearing their words but could not get my mind to process what they were saying. There had to be some mistake. I needed to wake up, and this would all go away. I was screaming inside: *No, NO, NO! You have to be wrong!*

As I sat there sobbing, the doctor asked if someone was on the way to be with me. I said yes, and asked that he please leave me alone.

The priest said, "Are you sure you want to be alone? Let me stay and comfort you."

"There's nothing you can do to comfort me. Please let me be alone." I sat there in the empty room for a few minutes and after some time—I don't know how long—the nun brought Amy back to me. The nun sat down next to me and asked if I needed anything.

Yeah, I do, but you can't give it to me.

She said that Amy had been asking a million questions and was worried. The nun said, "Amy wants to see Beth to make sure she's okay. I think you need to take her in to see Beth and explain to her what has happened. They've put her in a private room. Just you and Amy can go in."

I was horrified. "No! I can't take her in to see her."

The nun explained that I needed to talk to Amy and explain that Beth was gone, but how could I?

Beth can't be gone. Beth was never sick. It was Amy who had all the medical problems. Something is wrong here. Getting the brain to process that kind of information is like pushing a grapefruit through a straw. It just won't work. There is no way to explain it. It is so far away from any reality your mind will accept.

About that time my sister found us. When she came in and saw Amy with me, she was completely confused. We were still in the private waiting room, and I remember how small it was— maybe eight by ten feet with two small vinyl-covered couches. I sat down with Shelley to explain to her what had happened and take her through the last eighteen hours that led up to my little girl dying. Then as each family member arrived, I stood up to meet them and explain to each of them that no, it wasn't Amy, it was Bethany. And no, she was not seriously ill, she was gone. Within thirty minutes the room was crowded with people in shock and sobbing.

Not one of these people who loved Beth got there in time to say good-bye to her. I hadn't even been able to say good-bye.

●　　●　　●

I spent most of the rest of that morning comforting these poor people who had to deal with the shocking news as they arrived. I guess it was the easiest role for me to take—the caregiver once again—so I wouldn't have to confront my own horror. In the confusion of so many people coming in, a nurse had intercepted Steve's mom and step-dad in the hallway. Thinking they were aware of the circumstances, the nurse took them directly to the private room where Beth lay, looking like the sleeping angel that she actually was. That was how they found out that their granddaughter had died.

By midmorning, there were at least a dozen people in the tiny waiting room. Every twenty minutes or so, the nun or a nurse would come in and take a few people at a time to say good-bye to Beth. I couldn't go. If I walked in that room and saw her, it would be true. Finally the nun came in, sat down next to me, and took my hand in hers. She gently said, "They need to take Bethany away in a few minutes. It's time for you and Amy to go in and say good-bye."

I thought that was a terrible idea; I couldn't take this little six-year-old in to see her dead sister.

The nun tried to explain it to me. "You can't walk out of here without going in and seeing her. You need to have that closure, and so does Amy. If you let her leave the hospital thinking her sister is sick, she will never understand what's happened. It's important for both of you to go be with her. I will go with you if you'd like."

I got it then. She was right. I nodded. "No, it needs to be just the two of us."

I put Amy on my lap and tried to make her understand. "Amy, your sister can't be with us anymore. She was sick, but now she has died and is gone to heaven. We need to go tell her how much we love her and tell her good-bye."

Amy was confused, of course, "Mommy, what do you mean? She can't go away. She's my sister."

I took a deep breath and took Amy's hand as we walked into this room filled with sunshine. Beth was lying in a hospital bed looking like she was asleep. There was a yellow blanket all tucked in around her with her little arms on top on the blanket. We sat down beside the bed, and I tried to explain to Amy that she would never see her sister again, that Beth could not wake up. How could I find the words to explain to a six-year-old what I couldn't begin to understand? It broke my heart.

Amy asked me questions over and over. "Mommy, why can't

she wake up? Can she hear me? How long is she going to sleep? Can the doctor wake her up?"

I tried to answer each question as we sat and cried together. After a while I think she finally understood a little bit. She gently leaned over, took Beth's hand, and kissed her. She told her that she was the best sister ever, how very much she loved her, and to be good in heaven. "Don't wet your pants, and I'll miss you every day." It was the first glimpse I had that my daughter was an old soul sent here with the depth and wisdom that I had yet to learn.

I don't know how much time passed, but after a while the nurse came in and told us we needed to leave. As we walked out, there were two police officers waiting for me. They told me they needed to talk with me and took me into a private room and asked me questions for forty-five minutes. They wanted to know when Beth got sick, what she had to eat, if I took her to the doctor. They wanted every detail of the last twenty-four hours over and over again. The cause of death had not yet been determined; I guess this was standard procedure, but what an ugly way to end that horrible morning.

It was just after noon when we all started leaving the hospital. There was nothing left there to do. I think I must have been in shock when I told my sister that I was fine, I would drive. I needed to go to my friend Sandy's, to tell her we wouldn't be able to go to the zoo that day after all. Shelley tried to talk me out of it, but I insisted. I had not reached any place near reality yet. I just had to function so I wouldn't have to think and feel. Amy left with family members to go back to Steve's mom's as my sister and I drove to Sandy's.

Where was Steve in all of this? Well, he was still living in

California. I had tried to reach him all morning to tell him that Beth was very sick (a lie at this point), that she was probably going to be in the hospital for a few days, and that he needed to fly down. It happened that he was moving that day and in between phones in the house and the apartment he was moving to (before cell phones, of course) so I had not yet been able to reach him. I told his family members not to call him until I got to their house because he needed to hear this from me, not any of them. It was my job to tell him that the daughter I had taken away five weeks earlier was gone and he would never see her again.

As I left the hospital parking lot to drive across town to Sandy's, the first song that came on the radio was "My Special Angel," an old hit from the sixties. I will never forget that. Still I didn't fall apart. I was on automatic pilot, my brain and body still not processing what had just taken place. It's amazing how some things become a blur and others remain vivid in your memory. When we walked into Sandy's, her sister was there curling Sandy's hair. Sandy said she had been trying to call me to see what time we were going to the zoo. I started laughing. Laughing!

I said, "Sandy, we can't go to the zoo. Beth died this morning." Just like that—no prelude, no buildup. I just blurted it out and couldn't stop laughing at how absurd that was. They, of course, reacted like normal human beings and fell apart. They looked at me like I was insane, and for the moment I suppose I was. I don't remember how long we stayed.

As we left I said, "Oh, Sandy, would you call someone at work and tell them I probably won't be in on Monday." Later I found out that she called one of the managers from the radio station just after I left her house. He somehow managed to get the word to most of the people at the station.

We left Sandy's and drove to Steve's mom's house. My parents had been contacted by someone and were traveling back down from the Grand Canyon. I don't remember when they arrived. People were making phone calls and trying to reach family members to spread the news. I tried to call Steve every few minutes.

I finally reached him in the early afternoon. It was not easy to pull myself together and lie to him, but I could not tell him over the phone that his daughter had died. "Steve, I've been trying to reach you all day. Bethany is really sick, and I think you need to get on a plane and fly down here today."

He was confused and surprised. "Why didn't you call me last night?"

"Because I thought it was just the flu, and I didn't want to worry you," I lied.

He questioned me further. "What's wrong with her? What have the doctors said?"

"Steve, the doctor said she is seriously ill. They don't know what it is yet, but he asked me to call you. Please just get the next flight and get here."

I don't know how I pulled it off, but I couldn't tell him something so devastating when he was so far away. I made sure he understood that this was extremely serious, and then I got off the phone as quickly as possible. I think I was still functioning on autopilot and just said the words I'd rehearsed all morning.

When we found out his flight time, my sister and brother-in-law told me they would pick Steve up, but I insisted that I needed to go and break this news to him in person. My brother-in-law is a big guy, and he thought he might be needed when Steve was told. That turned out to be a smart decision. We drove to the airport and went outside to wait for his flight. In the seventies, passengers deplaned outside while we waited behind large glass retaining walls.

Steve was the first person off the plane. He came running across the tarmac. What I didn't realize or think about at the time was that when Steve saw me standing there, he knew without any words being spoken. If Beth was so sick, why was I at the airport and not at the hospital with her? I don't remember the words I said, but when he heard that his daughter had died that morning, he fell to his knees sobbing. It killed me to see his devastation.

After a few minutes of trying to find the words to explain and comfort him in some way, Bob helped him stand up. I thought he had calmed down, until Steve turned and put his fist through the six-foot glass window.

Somehow we got out of the airport without being arrested and got to Steve's mom's where we had to relive and retell the last twenty-four hours' events for Steve. He was, of course, shocked and completely distraught.

The next few days are very fuzzy. I remember moments, bits and pieces of conversations, something about arrangements for a funeral, but none of it is very clear. I don't even know who took care of all the details. I finally fell apart on Monday afternoon, sitting on the floor in the bedroom and sobbing with the reality of Bethany's death.

Steve and I were of no comfort to each other. I was filled with guilt, and he was trying to understand what had happened. Five weeks after we'd left California, he finally saw his daughter again Monday night, at the mortuary, in a casket. That is when reality hit him, and it took the form of anger at me. "If you hadn't left, this never would have happened. It's your fault that I'll never see my daughter again."

I took all of his anger and hurt and piled it on top of mine. Look what I had done. I thought my nightmare was almost too much to bear, but his must have been worse. He could barely sit next to me at the funeral the next day. He didn't speak to me unless it was necessary. We needed to support each other, but he couldn't find any love in his heart for me. I didn't blame him. I took it all in. Of course he was right, this was all my fault.

Amy was supposed to start first grade on Tuesday, August 30, in a brand-new school in a new city. Instead, she went to her beloved sister's funeral. I said earlier how strange memories are—parts very fuzzy, parts vividly clear. I remember I wore a rust-colored pantsuit the day Beth was buried, but I don't know what she wore. I refused to wear black, but I don't know if I picked out what I wore or if someone chose it for me. It was probably over 110 degrees that day, so it was going to be miserable no matter what we wore.

The services were held at Green Acres Cemetery in Scottsdale. As we pulled into the parking lot, I realized that it was full of cars. The first thing I noticed was a blue-and-white pickup with a camper on the back. It belonged to friends who had driven over from California to be there for us. I don't remember much of the service except for the part when the stranger standing up there talking about my daughter said she had died three days before her third birthday. I wanted to stand up and shout at him. Couldn't he even get the facts right? *She died three days after her birthday, not before, you idiot.*

There were hundreds of people there to say good-bye to Beth and support our family. I remember so many people coming up to us afterward, trying to express grief for something that no one can comprehend—the death of a child. I know the entire radio station was there. They had put a temporary announcer on the air and had a temporary receptionist handling the phones. Every employee was there—it amazed me. I remember people I hadn't seen in years walking up to me. I remember how devastated Cheryl, her preschool teacher, was. I remember Amy insisted on putting her Raggedy Ann doll in the casket so Beth wouldn't be lonely in heaven. I remember not being able to walk away from her casket at the internment and someone finally coming to get me as I stood alone. I remember that it meant more than words could ever express that all those people cared enough to come that day.

I had always thought funerals were barbaric and never understood their value. That day changed my mind. Funerals let the people who have to keep on living know that someone cares about them and they are there to support you in whatever small way they can. Now, matter how much I'd rather not, I will always go to a funeral to show those who have to go on that someone cares.

The rest of that day and next few days were hazy. I think people came back to Steve's mom's house, but I don't remember any of it. I think I took some medication that the doctor had given me, and maybe that's why most of those days are a blur; I don't know. A very close friend of mine had come down from northern California and stayed with me at the apartment. I don't know when Steve went back. I don't know when we cleaned out Beth's things. I don't know when I ate or when I slept or what I did with my days, except weep for hours and hours.

I do know that one or two days after the funeral, my parents got back into their RV and left again. I couldn't believe it. Did they think I would be just fine after a day or two? Years later I told my mom how much that hurt me. *How could you just leave me?* My mom had never been really good with emotional issues and would avoid any kind of sadness at all cost. She wouldn't even go to a movie if she thought there was a sad part in it. She said that she just "couldn't handle it" and had to get away. She told me that they went back to the Grand Canyon, and she sat out on a cliff and cried for hours and hours. I finally forgave her, but I have never understood it. I realize everyone handles grief differently; I guess she handled it in the best way she could.

●   ●   ●

Somehow, one day turned into the next, and after a week I went back to work. I remember walking down the hall from the back door and people just looking at me not knowing what to say. No one knows what to say to someone who has lost a loved one, especially a child. I went back on automatic pilot and tried to put people at ease with their discomfort.

I functioned somehow, but the pain was nearly unbearable. One hour turns into the next, and it's a milestone if you make it through a few hours without falling apart. Then if you make it until lunch. Three weeks later I still didn't know how to get through the day; two months later I still didn't know why she died.

The reports finally came in that Beth died of sepsis meningitis, a bacterial form of the disease that had somehow gotten into her bloodstream and shot-gunned it's way to her heart, her lungs, her liver, and several other organs in a matter of a few hours. It was a common bacteria that she could have picked up anywhere. One of the reasons that it hit her so hard was that she had never been sick as a baby and had not built up a strong immune system.

The doctors told me that if she had survived, she had so much damage to her vital organs that she would have lived her life in a vegetative state, never having the chance to lead a normal life. The knowledge did little to ease my pain.

Even harder than dealing with my own pain was seeing Amy's. She was so sad most of the time. Her first grade teacher would often call me at work to tell me she was having a very bad day and I needed to come get her. The times she did make it through the day, she would go to daycare afterward. Cheryl was a blessing. She watched Amy closely and gave her special love and attention. Then evening would come, and we would be back in our routine.

But it wasn't the same routine because Beth wasn't there. Amy refused to take a bath alone to the point that she would run outside and try to run away when it was bath time. She cried herself to sleep at night. I would sit with her trying to soothe her until she was exhausted. Then I would go to my room and stare at the ceiling and cry myself to sleep. One night as I lay in bed, I could hear her crying again. I went back into her room to try to give her some comfort.

When I got her calmed down enough to talk, she said, "Mommy, do you think we can get Beth to come back just for a few minutes? If God would let her come back for just a little while, I promise I'll let her go back, but I just need to check on her. What if she has an accident and wets her pants? Will she get in trouble? What if she wants peanut-butter-and-sweet-pickle sandwiches? Do they have those in heaven? Do they know how she likes the pickles sliced? I need to tell her to be good and that I love her. I promise I'll send her back."

My heart just broke into little pieces. How could I possibly explain such loss to a six-year-old when I could barely deal with it myself?

When I first decided to write about this, I thought maybe I could give someone else hope, to let them know that they can get through such a terrible loss. But I really don't have the answer. If someone asked me today how I got through it, I wouldn't know what to say. It's impossible—or at least is as close to impossible as it gets. Our brains and our hearts are just not built to withstand that kind of hurt, but somehow we do.

You keep breathing one moment at a time. I've come to realize that we each have a strength we never knew we had. When we need it, we can dig deep and find it. Somehow the moments run together and turn into hours and then into days, and you are still alive. You are constantly in pain, and it takes gargantuan strength to think about anything except your pain. The smallest task is monumental. You feel like you are always just a breath away from dying yourself, but somehow you keep going. You put one foot in front of the other, and you try to make it a few minutes longer, and you let your friends and family support you. You make a little progress, and then you have a major setback and try to recover and start again. You survive. Eventually you start to live again.

●　　　●　　　●

About three months after Beth died, I really didn't think I could cope with the loss. The pain in my chest each morning when I woke up was unbelievable. It was like an elephant standing on my chest, and I had trouble breathing. I didn't know emotional anguish could lead to such physical pain. I didn't sleep much at night. I would wake up in a panic in the middle of the night knowing something was wrong but not be able to figure it out for a second or two, and then it would come back to me. I was having anxiety attacks during the day. People suggested I see a counselor, but I couldn't afford it.

I woke up one night with such a strong anxiety attack I just couldn't stand it. I sat on my bed gulping in air and knew that I could not wake up again one more day and feel this much pain. I had felt that way for many days, but this time was different. I could not get through another day of this. I reached for the sleeping pills the doctor had given me and poured them all in my hand. It was somewhere around three o'clock in the morning, and as I sat there crying and trying to breathe, I didn't think about consequences. I just knew I couldn't do this another day.

For some reason I called my sister. She was sleepy and groggy when she answered the phone but instantly alert when she heard me sobbing. "Dee Dee, what's wrong? Has something happened? Take a breath and talk to me. You're scaring me."

I was hyperventilating and crying so hard I couldn't get words out at first. Shelley kept trying to get me to calm down, and finally I spoke through my sobs. "Shelley, I just can't do this anymore. I can't face another day hurting this much. I can't eat, I can't sleep, and it's too much. I just can't do this. You need to take care of Amy for me."

Shelley kept me on the phone while she let Bob know what was happening. He jumped in the car and raced to my apartment. In the meantime, she said, "Get up and go in and look at your other child. You love her so much, and she needs you now more than ever. Don't do this to her."

She kept at me until I finally walked in and looked at my beautiful sleeping daughter. Reality hit me in the face. Of course

I couldn't do this to her. By the time my brother-in-law got there, I was calm and rational again, but I will never forget that night. It was frightening to experience that level of desperation where nothing else mattered and nothing else was real except the pain I was in. Today I look back and think of all I would have missed if I had been successful. I don't believe suicide is the answer for anything, but I do understand how people can get to the point that they don't see any other way out.

●   ●   ●

So moment by moment Amy and I went on. We both had many days filled with tears. Amy would ask me endless questions about heaven and her sister. She worried about her so much. Thank God a child forgets those feelings. One of the most difficult periods for Amy, however, was when she did start forgetting. She came to me one day several months after Beth died, very upset. "I can't remember her face," she said.

We got out the photo albums again and looked at all the pictures of her sister. After that I made sure she had lots of pictures of Beth in her room, and I would often find them under her pillow.

They say time heals all wounds, and I suppose that's true. Maybe "heal" isn't the right word. The wound does close up a little bit, and it doesn't hurt as often. The pain, when it comes, is as strong as it was in the beginning, there are just more hours and days in between than there were in the beginning. Every hour becomes every day, and every day becomes a week, and then a month, and eventually you almost feel normal more often that you don't. You finally reach a point where the thoughts come less often, and you are able to deal with them better than you could last time. It's still remarkable to me that it is possible to go on and have a real life after losing a child, but it is.

Today, more than thirty years later, when I see a little girl with blond curly hair, I always see Beth. My heart skips a beat for just a moment. It doesn't hurt like it used to, but she's always around me in one way or another.

As my heart slowly healed, my memories faded, and that brought on a whole new set of anxieties. It's an awful feeling to have moments when you forget that you're supposed to be sad. I felt guilty if I laughed or had a few hours when I didn't think of Beth. I felt like I was betraying her. As time went by, it seemed like only a few of us remembered her, and that hurt as well. As much as I was trying to heal, it hurt when people quit mentioning her. People always think they should not bring up such a painful subject because they are afraid they'll make you cry. What those people don't realize is the hurt is still alive on the inside, it's just not erupting through your eyes at this moment. If you're not crying on the outside, you're probably crying on the inside anyway, and that is worse. It needs to be purged.

Years later, my mom, wanting to avoid the sadness she might have to deal with, made it a point to ignore Beth's birthday and the anniversary of her death. I finally had the nerve to talk to her about it and told her how much that hurt me. She told me she didn't want to make me sad by reminding me. *What, you think I forgot?*

I still get a strange feeling at the beginning of August. I know that her birthday and the anniversary of her death are coming up. In the first several years after she died, August was an awful time, and I spent the whole month building up anxiety. A black cloud would cover my world, getting darker and darker until "the week," and then the cloud would burst all over me. I would relive those excruciating days all over again. I finally learned to recognize the cloud when it first started building, and I've learned to deal with it. It took a very long time, but I try to celebrate her life instead of mourning her death.

The days around the twenty-fourth to the twenty-seventh of August will always be filled with thoughts of Bethany. Amy wants to hear stories, so we talk about her and get out the photo albums. I get through it, but I also know that it will never, ever go away completely. She was my child, and I will spend time with her every August.

Over the years it has become important to know that somebody besides me remembers her and acknowledges that she was my daughter, Amy's sister, and someone's granddaughter. She was here for three years—don't pretend that she didn't exist. That doesn't help. What helps is that years later on her birthday, someone says, "I just wanted you know I was thinking about Beth today." My sister has always understood this. Every year, for more than thirty years, I have received a card from Shelley on the anniversary of Bethany's death that always says, "I wanted you to know I was thinking of you and Amy and Beth today." I have all of those cards, and each one means more to me than I could ever express.

●   ●   ●

The first year was nearly unbearable—the first Halloween, the first Thanksgiving, the first everything. Christmas was a terrible time. While trying to make it a joyful time for Amy, Beth wasn't there. I didn't have very much money, but I knew I had to have Christmas for Amy. My mother-in-law gave us a little tabletop plastic tree because she knew I couldn't afford a big tree. We didn't have many ornaments, but I did have a few special ones that I had brought with us. Every year each we picked out a special ornament for each of the girls, and when we found the two that had been Beth's, Amy insisted on hanging them on our puny tree.

There was magic that Christmas though. One amazing act of love and kindness did more to help me get through it than anything else. My youngest brother, Jeff, played drums in a rock band that was on tour. He called me one morning in late December to say he had just arrived in town and wondered if he could use my apartment to relax for the afternoon.

"Sure, you need to come by work and get the key." I hadn't seen him for months, so I was excited to get the chance to see him.

When he got the key, he said, "I can't see you tonight because we're rehearsing, but we'll get together while I'm in town, I promise. I appreciate you letting me use your apartment. I just need to get a couple hours' sleep this afternoon, so I'm hiding from the rest of the family."

That evening, I picked up Amy from daycare after work and drove home as usual. When we walked in to our apartment, we both blinked and looked at each other. I wondered for a moment if we were in the wrong place. Standing across the room was a five-foot tall live Christmas tree all decorated with bows and popcorn and lights. Amy was so excited and thought I had surprised her. "Mommy, you got us a real tree!"

"No, Amy, I didn't do this."

"Mommy, do you think Santa brought it?" She jumped up and down with delight.

Just then I notice a white piece of paper stuck on one of

the branches. I walked over to read it and was overcome with emotion.

The note read, "Just look what a little love will grow. Merry Christmas. Love, Santa Jeff."

It wasn't the most gorgeous tree you've ever seen. The decorations were not fancy, but it was beautiful to me. When I called my brother to thank him, he just said, "Dee Dee, it's the least I can do. That little plastic tree was awful. You and Amy deserve a real Christmas." It was the sweetest thing he could have possibly done.

Bethany's next birthday, with the anniversary of her death just three days later, was the worst. Steve and I needed to continue to be parents to Amy, but Beth's death changed us so deeply. In his anguish he would call me and rage at me for taking his daughter away from him, and I would take it because I felt so guilty. "If only" plagued me to the bottom of my soul. If only I hadn't left him. If only I had called the doctor sooner, taken her directly to the hospital. If only, if only …

I had so much guilt, I didn't think I was worth the air I needed to breathe and that I deserved every awful thing he said to me. I felt that way for a very long time.

CHAPTER SIX

1980 Time Moves On

Amy healed faster than me, as children do. Somewhere along the line, she decided she needed to be the parent in this relationship. I don't know if she was born this way, if it was because of all that she had been through with her medical history, or losing her sister—probably all three—but she was trying to raise me right. She would call me at work to remind me that it was Girl Scout night and I needed to sew the latest patch on her uniform before that night's meeting. She would tell me to stop at the store on the way home and get milk and eggs, or not to forget my dentist appointment. She would try to do nice things for me, like washing my silk blouses. (That didn't work so well.) We became a team supporting each other, but I think she was the one that kept things together.

In the fall of 1979, about two years after Beth died, a friend of mine at work was worried about me. I was doing a little better at coping with the loss of Beth, but I was not doing very well with the guilt. He decided what I needed was a man in my life, so he introduced me to his friend Jim. Jim the cop.

Jim was—is—one of the nicest people you'd ever want to meet. A big, tall man with a full head of grey curly hair, he wasn't especially handsome, but he had warm eyes that lit up when he smiled. I knew right away that he was genuine and kind with a gentle, huge heart. So we became friends.

Jim had three sons, and it turned out that he lived less than a block away from me. We would meet in the park and let the kids play or come up with some kind of activity for them. Amy loved Jim, and she loved having the three boys in her life. We started dating, and the relationship grew. I think I needed someone to lean on so badly. Jim was good to me. He would sit and listen to stories about Beth for hours and hours. He would ask me to tell him about her over and over, and I believe this was one of the most important parts of my healing.

I finally came to understand that carrying around all of those painful feelings was an enormous energy drain. It took up so much space in my heart and head that it took away my ability to move forward. I needed to find a way to let it go, and talking was the way that worked for me.

Amy was eight, and Jim's youngest boys were ten-year-old twins. They all liked each other immediately. Jimmy, the oldest, was a young teenager. He wasn't too sure about my dating his dad in the beginning, but Jimmy and I eventually formed a great bond. Jim and I had great times taking the kids to the park or to the movies. When we didn't have the kids with us, Jim took me out to nice dinners, ball games, movies—things I hadn't been doing at all for two years. So Jim and I got closer. He pulled me out of the deep dark place I'd been in and made me laugh again. All he wanted was to make me happy, and he did everything he could to get me to a better place. So in the spring of 1980, less than a year after meeting him, I decided to show him how grateful I was by marrying him. Poor guy—we never had a chance.

Jim was the saver, and I needed to be saved. As long as we were in those roles, we were good, but it's not a great foundation for a marriage. Jim helped me find the strength to become a person again and by doing so put our marriage in jeopardy. As I grew stronger, our relationship grew weaker. The foundation that our marriage was built on was slipping away. I don't know if it was Jim's personality or cop mentality, or a combination, but within a year of being married, I realized Jim had some personality traits I really didn't like.

Jim was good when he was in the role of "taking care of" or "fixing." But if I showed some independence or wanted to make some decisions, he was not happy. This became truly clear to me at the end of our marriage. I was up for a big promotion at work, and he was against it. He thought I'd have to work too hard, I would travel too much, it was too much stress.

"Why don't you just go back to being a secretary? I'll take care of you."

I know it sounds nice to think about someone taking care of you, but there was a different tone to this offer. It was about my staying dependent and needy when I needed to get strong. This was about holding me back. Jim saved people, and he had saved me. But when we were on equal footing, it wasn't right between us. That's when I knew we were headed in very different directions. As I grew stronger, we argued more. I started realizing I had married Jim for all the wrong reasons. I really didn't love him the way he deserved.

We had been together three years, and I knew this was not how I could spend the rest of my life. After we split up, most of my friends and family told me that they knew from the start that this relationship would not last but didn't have the heart to tell me. For a long time, I looked at that marriage as a mistake, but it was not a mistake. Jim saved me and helped me get my life back. When I knew I needed to move on, I took Amy out to dinner to try to explain why our life was going to change again. I told her that I had made a mistake marrying Jim, and I was so sorry to hurt her, but the marriage was going to end.

She said, "Mom, did you love Jim when you married him?"

"Yes, I did. I just wasn't in a very good place in my life yet."

"Mom, it wasn't a mistake. It was right at the time. Don't feel bad."

Thanks Amy, my wise little twelve-year-old.

●   ●   ●

Amy and I found a cute little townhouse to live in, and we started building a life for just the two of us. I was making ends meet and we were moving on. My work continued to grow and improve at the radio station. I became an assistant to the national sales manager, and after a few years I was recruited by another station to be their national sales manager—an incredible opportunity. I was concerned about handling the job and still being the mom that Amy needed. I went home one day to talk with her about it. I wanted this chance, but it meant traveling. I had promised myself that being a mom would come first, career would come second, and I didn't know what kind of effect this job would have on our lives.

One evening after dinner, I asked Amy to come sit down beside me on the sofa. She was nearly thirteen and therefore immediately was suspicious that she was in trouble for something. "Uh-oh, what did I do?" she asked.

I laughed and said, "You didn't do anything wrong. I have a very important decision to make, and I want to talk to you about it."

I explained a little about the job and what changes it would make for us. "This job is pretty big. It means I might have to work late some nights, and I will have to travel out of town a few times a year."

"Where do you have to go, and how long will you be gone?"

"I'll have to go to Chicago and New York, and maybe a few other cities once or twice, but I'll never be gone more than a night or two."

"Well, that's okay," she answered. "I can always stay with Dad or Aunt Shelley or Grandma and Grandpa, right?

"Absolutely," I assured her.

"Could you ever take me with you on a trip? Like maybe to New York?"

"That's something we could work on. I can't promise, but maybe."

She thought about it for a minute and then stated, "Okay, I have another question. Do you know if you'll ever get this opportunity again?"

"Well, no, I don't know for sure."

"You have to take it then. We'll make it work, Mom. How would you feel if you passed this up and then never got another chance?"

So I took the job, and we adjusted to our new schedule. I only traveled a few times a year, and there was plenty of family to take care of Amy. By this time Steve had married again, and we were able to put the pieces of a friendship back together—at least enough to be parents. He was now living in Phoenix, and he said he'd be there for her, so together we made it work.

Amy was far from perfect, however. When she was thirteen, she met a boy at church that she started talking about a lot. I had not met him, but I heard his name popping up in the conversation a little too often. One night I was in bed reading when Amy came in and sat on the end of the bed. "Mom, Jesse wants to know if I can ride the bus over to his house Saturday."

I don't think so. "Ride the bus? Absolutely not," I replied.

She argued a while and finally, defeated, went back in her room. She came back in about ten minutes later with a different approach. "Well, what if Sadaari goes with me?"

"No."

She retreated and came back for one more try.

As she started losing that battle too, she said, "It's not fair. You teach me too stand up for myself and fight for what I want, and the minute I do you shoot me down."

I said, "You're right. You showed excellent effort and put up a good argument, but this isn't a democracy. End of discussion."

She wasn't very happy with me, but I have to say she really did show good negotiating skills.

Most of the time Amy was such a good girl and an easy child to raise that it was startling when she turned thirteen and morphed into an alien I did not recognize. Why didn't someone warn me? She'd gone to bed one night as sweet as always and walked out of her room the next morning with attitude and raging hormones. If she didn't get her way, she sulked around the house and made sure anyone in her path knew how miserable her life was. She argued with me and became defiant. On more than one occasion, she slammed doors and yelled, "I hate you!" at the top of her lungs.

Who are you and what have you done with my daughter? Good grief, what do I do with this monster who has taken over my life, my home, and my sanity? She was impossible! She was a teenager!

My sister tried to spend as much time as she could with Amy and often invited her to go on family camping trips. Shelley called me that summer to ask if Amy wanted to go again.

I answered quickly, "Yes, she does. How soon are you leaving?"

They went camping, and I got a few days of peace and quiet. When they returned I asked Amy if she had a good time; she'd always had a great time on past trips. This time, she gave me the "it was fine" answer. I was afraid to call Shelley and ask what that might mean, so when Shelley called a few days later, I asked her about the trip.

"Oh, it was fine."

"That's all? Just fine?" I asked.

She stammered around a little bit and then said, "Uh, have you noticed a change in Amy lately? She just wasn't the same this year."

I laughed. "Oh yes, I've noticed. I was afraid if I told you what a brat she's become, you wouldn't take her, and I needed the break. She's going through adolescence. It's just not pretty is it?"

Shelley said, "No, not at all. Let me know when it's over. I'll see her again then."

I laughed again. "Call back when she's eighteen."

●   ●   ●

So Amy and I had started the teenage years. We tried to find ways to maneuver through this part of the journey without killing each other. We had some good days and we had some bad days; our relationship was certainly being tested. But we were close, and I knew we'd get to the other side eventually.

Then came Black Monday—a day I had seen coming for a while. I knew I was not going to like this conversation when Amy said, "Mom, we need to talk."

Uh-oh. Okay, whatever it is, I can handle it like the mature adult I am supposed to be.

Then she followed up with, "Now, I don't want you to take this personally, this is not about you. This is about Dad. I want to live with him."

Oookaaay, breathe slowly, in and out, repeat often. I mean, things were rough between us, but was I ready for this?

I thought the best way to handle this maturely was to just sit there and not speak. I didn't trust the words that might come out at the moment. Looking back, I think I did handle it quite well. I did not run around the room screaming, or throw myself on the floor, or throw up on the couch. I just sat there, feeling a dull knife twist in my heart. With anyone else, that might have worked, but once again, the logical, practical child was my downfall.

She waited until I was breathing normally and then explained very simply, "I just want to know my dad better. Is that bad?"

What a con. One that I fell for, hook, line, and sinker. I could not fight her wanting to be a part of her dad's life. In my head, I thought she was pretty great for wanting to spend more time with her dad. My emotions, on the other hand, were doing a swan dive into a black hole. All right, so I'm not too quick. It took me a while to figure out that she just thought she could get away with more cause "Daddy was easy" and I was too strict. Oh boy, was the joke on her!

In the few weeks before she moved, Amy went above and beyond the call of duty, showering me with attention and affection. On the Saturday she moved out, I was pretty proud of my behavior. Although I really didn't think I could survive, I decided I could be as adult about this as she could. I was still under the belief that she had weighed the issues and made a very mature decision. I would not heap pounds of guilt upon her very young shoulders for leaving me. (Oh, but when she called after she got the first "No! You cannot go out with a boy!" from her dad, I did have a good private laugh.)

I was brave and courageous as I helped her pack her things. When she was ready to go, she assured me of her love and devotion and that she would always be there for me when I needed her. The minute she was out the door, I went to bed and stayed there for forty-eight hours.

I survived Monday at work by pretending nothing had changed. Then it was six o'clock, and as I walked into my house, I was overwhelmed with its emptiness. What did single adults do in the evening? I had no idea how to pass the time if I wasn't sewing Girl Scout badges, keeping score at a ball game, listening to giggly girls talk about stupid boys, or pleading for five minutes of phone time. After changing my clothes, feeding the cat, watering the plants, and staring at her empty room, I still had two hours and forty-five minutes to fill before the ten o'clock news. I had not had that amount of time all to myself for as long as I could remember. I was totally lost.

On Tuesday, I was coerced into joining a group of people from work in the great American singles pastime: happy hour. I knew I would have to find something else to fill my time, because I couldn't afford this every night, but it at least took care of Tuesday. Then came Wednesday. I had not been looking forward to Wednesday, but it was coupon day, and I was out of groceries, so I had no choice. Walking along the aisle of single-serving frozen dinners was painful, but when I got to the mac and cheese section, I lost it. I stood in the middle of the aisle with big tears streaming down my face. I was trying hard to be strong, but the mac and cheese did me in. Good grief. I was nearly forty years old and couldn't grocery shop by myself. I had become dependent on my daughter, and I didn't know how to function without her. I missed her so much. I was so embarrassed; I quickly turned and ran out of the store.

As I walked to the car, I started laughing. *Oh, come on, I can do this. I have to do this.* Someone had spent a lot of time teaching Amy about surviving and being independent, self-sufficient, and responsible, and I think it was me. Surely I could remember some of those things. I had to learn to live life on my own, whether I liked it or not, so I might as well get started.

That day was a turning point. I've laughed and cried about it many times. Soon after that night, I discovered a new adult world of exercise, movies, books, plays, dinner parties, and even dates. It wasn't always easy, and there were many setbacks along the way. My first date without Amy there to check my wardrobe and calm my nerves was traumatic. But I got through it. There were many days when she wasn't there and I needed a hug that only a daughter can give a mother, but we saw each other often and did lots of verbal hugging in between. Steve and I had even reached the point where we could spend time together and made a point to have some family adventures.

We both adjusted and starting leading healthy, happy lives. It didn't happen overnight, and I don't know how I'd have turned out had I not been blessed with Amy to help me find my way. She was growing into a wonderful semi-adult person finding her own way. Our relationship continued to get better and better and became clearly defined. She let me be the parent most of the, time and I let her make out my grocery list every once in a while. Today, while we certainly don't agree on everything, we are special friends who love and respect each other all the time. The truth is, we are complete opposites. I don't know how that happens, but we are about as different as two people can be. Somehow, we get past all that and truly share unconditional love.

D —— CHAPTER SEVEN

1986 Joy and Healing

Nearly twenty years after giving up my first child, I was blessed to be able to experience adoption from the other side, and it finally healed the hole in my heart. My sister Shelley and her husband Bob had tried for years to have children. She was an elementary school teacher, and she and Bob both loved children so much. They wanted a baby more than anything in the world.

Shelley and I were very close, and I knew how difficult it was for her not to be able to conceive a child. She would call me nearly every month in tears, telling me, "Not this month." He voice was always so filled with disappointment and heartache. They had gone to doctor after doctor, and I don't think they ever got a solid diagnosis as to why they couldn't conceive.

After ten years, they finally decided that adoption was the only way they would have a child. They spent months and months going through all the procedures necessary to make that happen. And then they waited. They would get a phone call from their attorney telling them there might be a baby available soon, and then it would fall through. It was a terrible emotional roller coaster for them.

One Saturday my phone rang, and Shelley told me that their attorney had called again saying she might have a baby for them. It wasn't a sure thing, and Shelley was reluctant to share the news that might result in nothing, but she could not keep it to herself. The following Tuesday they got the call that told them they were one of two couples being considered for a brand new baby boy. They could be parents within twenty-four hours. The next morning my sister called: "It'sgoingtohappen.Theypickedus. We'regoingtogethim."

"What? Shelley slow down and speak English! Tell me what's happening."

She took a couple of slow, deep breaths and then started again. "The lawyer called. The baby is ours! We're going to be parents at two o'clock this afternoon." She was barely able to speak, she was filled with so much emotion. I was so excited for them, but it brought back so many memories and made my pain fresh again. I didn't want to let my emotions spoil this wonderful time but, it was difficult not to think about my son.

Shelley said, "Come over as soon as you can! You have to be here."

I said, "Are you sure? Don't you and Bob want to be alone with your new baby?"

She cried, "No! I don't know what to do, and Bob's more nervous than I am. You have to come help."

"Okay, okay." I laughed. "We'll get there as soon as we can."

Amy and I quickly got dressed, jumped in the car and headed to the closest mall. We ran in the first department store we found and bought every baby thing in sight and then threw everything in the trunk of our car and raced to their house.

When we pulled up in front of their house, the first thing we saw was a large sign in the middle of the front yard with "Welcome Home Scott" painted in big, bold letters. There were blue balloons tied to the car, the front porch, and the patio chairs. Inside, it was much the same. The living room was filled with balloons, a basinet, and baby toys. My brother in-law sat quietly on the couch biting his fingernails. After bringing in our haul, I found my sister in the kitchen. She looked beautiful, dressed in a pretty white cotton summer dress, her long blond hair in curls. She was furiously mopping the kitchen floor.

I said, "Shelley, I don't think your baby's going to care that the floor is dirty, but would you like me to do that for you?" She said she was too nervous to sit still and continued mopping away. Two o'clock came and went, with each tick of the clock sounding like a bomb going off. At two fifteen, she just knew there had been a disaster of some kind, and by two thirty she was nearly hysterical.

Finally, at two forty we heard car doors closing and voices outside. We ran outside to greet the lawyer and the social worker who pulled this tiny infant out of the car. Shelley was shaking so hard we were certain she would drop the baby, and Bob was no better, so the social worker carried baby Scott into the house. The attorney made Shelley sit on the couch before she would hand the baby over because she didn't think Shelley would be able to hold him standing up.

That moment will be vivid in my memory forever. As the lawyer placed Scott in her arms, huge tears rolled down her cheeks splashing on his tiny bald head. Within a short period of time, the entire contingent of grandparents, aunts, uncles, and neighbors arrived. It was standing room only, but you could have heard a pin drop. We all stood around in the living room just watching Shelley and Bob sitting on the couch together holding the baby. The baby was asleep, and we just stared at him. No one had words and they weren't necessary. The picture of that family who had waited so long for their son told the story. It was one of the most special moments of my life. It is rare to experience such incredible joy, to see so many years of wanting and love finally fulfilled. We were all overcome with emotion, and I was experiencing something I thought would never happen: healing.

When I gave my child away so many years earlier, it never entered my mind to consider what was happening on the other side. I was dealing with too much sadness and despair to think about the adoptive parents. As I stood and watched my sister experience the closest thing she ever would to childbirth, I realized what joy I had given to some couple just like them. I cried a little harder than some of the others in that room, but it was very different from all the tears I had shed in the past. Although I would always feel emptiness, I felt released from years of torment and guilt and got to experience what a very special gift I had given someone else.

Relatives came over for the next several hours, and Shelly never got up off the couch. I think she may have let Bob hold the baby for a while, but I'm not even sure. We prepared food and made sure they were well stocked with all the supplies they would need for the next few days, because it was obvious they wouldn't be going anywhere! That evening I knew it was time for Amy and me to leave and let them have their child to themselves, so I got ready to go. Instead of happily kicking us out, they both panicked.

"Oh, please don't leave us," Shelley cried. "We have no idea what to do. Can't you stay overnight?" I laughed and told her there wasn't a new mom on the planet that knew what to do, but I couldn't move in. She might as well start figuring it out now.

The next morning my phone rang at six thirty. It was Shelley on the phone sobbing.

"Oh my God, what's wrong?" I yelled.

Through sobs she very slowly said, "It's not a dream. He's still here. I can't believe he's still here." After an agonizing six months of waiting for final approval from the court, Scott E was truly their son.

I have to admit that through all this joy, I couldn't help but think about my son and wondered where he was, what he was doing, what kind of family he had. Was he happy? But I thought about him and wondered about him every day anyway. To see the joy of two parents receiving such an amazing gift didn't make those thoughts go away, but it somehow made them a little easier to deal with. It gave me a way to get out of my own sadness and see the other side.

— CHAPTER EIGHT

1988 California, Here I Come

For the next couple of years I drifted along on my own. About six months earlier I had taken a job at a new TV station in town. I thought that changing from radio to TV would be exciting, but it wasn't. Everything in my life was just okay—not bad, but not great either. Although I don't think it was the walk in the park Amy expected, living with her dad seemed to be working out pretty well. I missed her constantly, but her life with Steve was good. She got very involved with a church group throughout high school and stayed on a positive path.

I slowly started to realize that my life was pretty empty. I was spending too much of my free time sitting in bars with my single girlfriends. I was forty years old, in a job I didn't love, and going nowhere fast. I started thinking about making some changes in my life. I was ready to have a fresh start.

About that same time, we started noticing some serious changes in my mom and dad. They lived out in the desert, easily a thirty-minute drive north of town, and spent summers at their cabin in Idaho, so whenever any of us saw them it was a planned visit. We didn't just drop by unexpectedly. That fall, when they came back after being at their cabin all summer, my mom looked awful: tired, drawn, and unkempt. It was out of character; my mom was a beautiful redhead, a vibrant, very stylish woman. My dad's behavior was getting bizarre as well. He was often angry at the smallest, most insignificant things. He seemed out of sorts, but there was nothing specific. I wrote it off to old age. I didn't understand there was much more to it than that.

You know that old saying, "If you want to hear God laugh, just tell him your plans." I had been giving more thought to making some big changes in my life and was seriously considering moving away. Amy was a senior in high school and would continue living with her dad until she was on her own, so that wasn't an issue. Just as I started making some preliminary plans, I got the phone call on a Monday afternoon that changed everything.

I was at my desk at work when Aunt Lee, my mom's sister, called. "Dee Dee, I just got off the phone with your dad. There's something wrong at their house. You need to get out there right away."

"Lee, slow down. What are you talking about? What do you mean something's wrong?"

"Your dad answered the phone, and I asked to talk to your mom. He said no, she couldn't come to the phone. I asked him why, and he said she had fallen down and was hurt."

"What?" I cried. "What do you mean, she's hurt?"

"I don't know; he wouldn't say. He wasn't making any sense, and he hung up on me. I don't know what's going on. How fast can you get out there?"

"I'm on my way," I replied. "I'll get there as fast as I can. Call

Shelley and tell her to get out there too. She can probably get there faster than me."

"Okay, I will," she said. "And please call me as soon as you can."

"I will. Bye." And I was out the door.

I drove like a maniac, covering the forty miles in record time. When I walked in the door, Mom was lying on the couch, and I could see a big bloody gash on the side of her head. She was barely awake, couldn't form sentences, and was completely out of it. Dad was sitting in the chair crying, and I could not get him to make any sense at all. I was sure Mom had suffered a stroke.

My sister arrived just minutes after I did. We both were perplexed and worried. We quickly made a little bed in the back of Shelley's van then carried Mom outside and got her settled. They lived so far out, it would have taken longer for an ambulance to get there. We just needed to go.

As we started to leave, my dad started exhibiting even stranger behavior. He said he was afraid to leave the house, but he didn't want us to leave him alone.

"Dad, we have to leave and get Mom to the hospital. You either have to come with us or stay here. We'll call you as soon as we can."

He cried some more, which was completely unsettling for Shelley and I. "Will you bring me a blanket so I can lie on the couch while you're gone?"

I ran to the bedroom and found a blanket for him. "Dad, we'll be back, but we've got to go now. We're taking Mom for stitches."

He was a seventy-year-old man; surely he could look after himself for a few hours.

We made sure Mom was resting comfortably in the back of the Shelley's van and raced toward the hospital. As we were driving, my sister said she thought she had smelled liquor on my mom's breath, but I knew that couldn't be true. Mom had quit drinking a couple of years earlier. She had recently developed some palsy-type symptoms and some severe stomach problems. She had been seeing a doctor over the last few months. We were afraid she had Parkinson's disease.

We were flying down a remote road on the outskirts of town, going at least ninety miles an hour, when all of a sudden the hood of the Shelly's van flew up, hit the windshield and shattered it! It scared the hell out of both of us, and we had to pull over to the side of the road. We got the hood back down a little bit, but it was twisted and broken so it wouldn't close all the way. We limped down side of the road with both of us looking out the side windows to see where we were going. (How did we manage before cell phones?)

We made it to Shelley's house, got Mom out of the van and settled into another car, and zoomed off. We arrived at the hospital in the late afternoon and sat for hours while they had her in the emergency room doing tests. We called all the family members we could find and waited.

Finally, around midnight, nearly six hours after we arrived, they let us in to see her. She was able to speak and recognize us. As we stood at her bedside, the doctor came in to the room. I'll never forget how shocked I was at what he had to say. "Your mom's blood tests are back, and I'm afraid the only thing wrong with her is that she is highly inebriated. Her blood alcohol content is extremely high."

I looked at him with astonishment and indignantly said,

"That's ridiculous! You've obviously made a mistake and have someone's else's results. My mother doesn't drink."

He said, "I'm sorry but there's no mistake. These are your mother's results, and I'm surprised she doesn't have alcohol poisoning. She has consumed a very large amount of alcohol."

"But she hasn't had a drink for months," I responded angrily. "You are wrong." I was furious at their stupidity, told him to rerun the tests, and let him know just what I thought.

Mom was lying there awake and said, "Dee Dee, calm down, please don't yell at the doctor. There's no need to run more tests." I just stared at her. "He's right," she said. "I'm so sorry. You and Shelley come over here, and I'll try to tell you what happened today."

We were relieved and grateful that it wasn't a stroke, but more than anything we were shocked—beyond shocked. This was our mom! She then started explaining what had gone on that day. She started to tell us a story that I wouldn't have believed if I hadn't been sitting next to her in the hospital.

"There's been something wrong with your dad for quite a long time, and I don't know what it is. His behavior just get's stranger and stranger, and he's driving me crazy. He asks me questions over and over again, he forgets where he puts things, he follows me around constantly. He's making me crazy." She went on to tell us that she really thought he was losing his mind, and while trying to cope with him and hide it from us, she had started drinking to get through the day. Just a little, to help her cope. But the little sip started a little earlier every day. After a while she knew it was out of hand, but she couldn't deal with him.

She told us some of the things he was doing: Peeing into the plants on the patio instead of in the bathroom. Taking food from the refrigerator and hiding it all over the house. Yelling at her if she caught him doing something out of the ordinary. She said he would get so mad if he got caught, she was afraid he might hit her.

She went on. "He gets up in the middle of the night and wanders around the house and sometimes outside. Sometimes he tries to get the keys and leave in the car in the middle of the night."

She said she thought she had been drinking all day and fell against the fireplace and hit her head then passed out. My dad was in such a bad state that he didn't even know how to help her or call anyone for help. He just left her there on the floor.

By this time, Shelley and I were both in tears, not to mention horrified at the things Mom was telling us.

"Mom, why haven't you said anything before? Why haven't you told us what's been going on?" I tearfully asked.

"I thought I could handle it, and then I didn't want you to know about the drinking. I don't know why. I just didn't want to burden any of you."

Shelley asked, "How long has this been going on?"

Mom looked at us. "The drinking or your dad?"

"Both," Shelley replied.

My mom—who doesn't cry—had tears in her eyes. "Too long. Maybe as long as a year. When we were up at the cabin in Idaho over the summer, it was easy to hide it. But it started a long time before we left last spring." By this time she was exhausted and having a hard time staying awake again.

The doctor asked us to step out in the hall for a moment so he could talk with us further. "I don't know what's all is going on here, but it sounds to me like your mom has a serious drinking problem and needs some help."

Shelley and I were dumbfounded. *This is our mom you're talking about. What is happening here?*

He said, "I have to release her, but I can suggest some people for you to talk to tomorrow."

"Release her?" I yelled. "You can't release her! She needs to be here."

"No, she really doesn't. There's nothing wrong with her except that she needs to sober up some more."

We begged the doctor to keep her overnight so we could figure out what to do. It was well after midnight, and we still needed to drive back out and tell Daddy what was going on. We'd been gone more than six hours, and after what Mom had just told us, he probably shouldn't be alone for six minutes.

The doctor finally relented and said he would keep her until morning, but that was all. We left the hospital and made the long drive back out to Mom and Dad's house. It was the middle of the night when we arrived, and when we walked in the door, Dad was still in the same place we left him with his blanket on his lap. He was very disoriented and didn't know where Mom was.

We brought him back in to my sister's and put him to bed and then spent what was left of the night talking about what to do. Bob was waiting for us when we finally settled at her kitchen table. He worked in the pharmaceutical industry and spent a lot of time around doctors, so he was pretty knowledgeable. He was a huge help in getting us to face reality when we both wanted to be in denial about what was going on. We finally all agreed to go back to the hospital the next morning to tell Mom that we believed she had a serious drinking problem, and she was going into rehab whether she liked it or not. We were prepared for a fight.

When we walked into the hospital the next morning and saw her, it was the saddest sight. She was in restraints because she had the tremors so badly. She told us more about how Dad had been acting strangely for months, and she would have a little drink once in a while just to give herself a little relief. But as he got worse, so did her drinking. She admitted she was in trouble and would do whatever we wanted to get help. She was worried about how Dad would get along without her but agreed to check into a rehab facility that day. What a relief.

We got her admitted and then started trying to figure out what was going on with him. We took him to various doctors and found out he had substantial dementia, most likely Alzheimer's disease, and needed constant supervision. This was in the late eighties, and I had never heard of Alzheimer's disease. Boy, did we have a lot to learn.

●　　●　　●

Dad moved in with my sister. She lived the closest to their house and had the most room. I put my plans to move on hold, and we all spent the next six weeks trying to help both parents get through this terrible time. We spent many hours babysitting Dad and going through family counseling with Mom. It was terribly difficult to sit there and watch my mom—who I had always thought was a superhero in disguise—admit she was an alcoholic at the age of sixty-five.

One of my mom's favorite sayings is that "something good always comes out of something bad," and it's true even if you have to look pretty hard sometimes. One of the silver linings from

Mom's rehab was that my oldest brother, Ron, finally owned up to his alcoholism. It had been ruling his life for years, probably since he was a teenager, but he had not reached the point that he would believe or admit it.

One day we had a family session at Mom's treatment facility. All the family members were invited to participate and talk about their feelings in dealing with their loved ones. All five of us kids were there and walked into this large room about the size of a gymnasium. There were a few rows of chairs in a U shape all around the outside of the room. When we walked in, there were probably thirty people already seated, so we found seats together near the back. At the other end of the room was one chair for the counselor who would lead this group.

"This is your opportunity to address your questions, voice your concerns, and generally share your experiences to try to help each of you understand the rehabilitation process better." He went from family to family asking them questions, letting them express their emotions, and helping them find ways to deal with the challenges they were facing. There were parents of teenage drug abusers, there were sisters and brothers, husbands and wives, all there because someone they loved was abusing alcohol or drugs. There were no other adult children there to deal with their mom's alcohol problem.

Toward the end of the session, the therapist asked Ron why he was so angry. Ron was not participating, and he voiced his opinion that this whole process was bullshit. He gave the therapist some smart-ass answer, but the therapist wouldn't let him off the hook and kept at him. Ron just sat down with his arms crossed over his chest. You could practically see the steam coming out of his collar. He didn't say a word for two hours.

When the session was almost over, Ron suddenly stood up. The room got silent but no words came out for a while. Finally he said, "I have something to say."

The therapist told him to go ahead.

After a few more minutes, Ron very slowly said, "I am an alcoholic."

Everyone in the room stood and applauded his courage. I think sitting in that session was the first time Ron truly realized his alcohol problem, or at least the first time he admitted it. A few days later, he flew back to his home in Boise, Idaho, and started his road to recovery. He has been clean and sober ever since and has participated heavily Alcoholics Anonymous, helping hundreds of others with their addiction.

When we were kids, sometimes Ronny would beat me up. He and I grew up not liking each other very much. It wasn't until after his rehab process, when we were both adults, that we found friendship and I discovered what a fine human being was under all of the insecurity. Not until he was an adult did we all realize that he suffered from several learning disabilities all through school. The term "learning disabilities" didn't exist when he was a child, so he struggled through school, and maybe because of his many years of frustration, became the bad boy.

In the years since his sobriety, I've gotten to know my brother. I found this incredibly warm, intelligent, loving, and giving human being who was nothing like the person I had known as a child. Since then I identify my brother by before and after his rehab. The guy I grew up with is *Ronny,* and *Ron* is the brother I love now.

Another lesson I learned while Mom was in rehab turned out to be life changing for me. At the family sessions, we were all supposed to talk about our feelings and experiences dealing with this process. One Saturday morning, we had been sitting in this group for a very long time listening to other families. When the therapist came to us, he asked me about my feelings. I stepped into my good girl role, of course, and started talking about my concern for my mom. He asked, "How do you feel about your mom being here?"

I replied, "I'm happy she's here, but it is still hard for me to believe. I just want her to get better. I'll do whatever I need to do to help."

He said, "Yes, but how do you feel?"

I wasn't quite sure how to respond. "Well, I'm sad and worried, I guess."

He stopped me and said, "But what about your anger? Aren't you angry at her for doing this? This is your mom we're talking about." He kept pushing. "You must be mad at her for all she's putting you through."

I started to get upset and found all kinds of emotions bubbling to the surface. I started crying and said, "No, I'm not angry. I'm just tired."

He kept asking me questions and finally I blurted, "I just can't do it all! I can't come here to see her every day and take care of my daughter, and work, and take care of my dad and get him to the doctors," and who knows what else I threw in there.

He quietly looked at me. "Who said you have to do it all?"

"There's nobody else to do it! Everybody else is too busy or they won't take the time. It's all up to me."

He let me rant on for a while and then hit me with a crucial question, "What makes you think you are so almighty important?"

What? What? I was pissed!

"It's not about that," I yelled. "It just always all falls on me."

"Dee Dee, you are not that effing important, you just think you are."

By this time I was sobbing and outraged. How could he humiliate me like that in front of all those people? I just turned and ran out the door, found a place to sit outside, and cried, letting it all come out.

When the session ended, he came looking for me. He sat down next to me and said, "I'm sorry if I hurt your feelings, but I want you to see what you're doing. You are taking all these burdens on yourself and then resenting that you have to do them. It's going to make you bitter and angry. You don't have to do it this way. There are other people to do these things with you and for you. You just won't ask for help, because then you won't feel so important. Think about it."

I think about those words all the time. He was absolutely right. I do have the tendency to take on too much and not ask for help or at least I used to. When I find myself heading in that direction now, I remember that day clearly and remind myself that I don't have to take it all on to feel important. There are other people out there, and all I have to do is ask. My most important life rule was born that day, although it took me a long time to recognize it: If you choose it, don't bitch. Isn't that simple? It is such a good rule and it works, at least for me. Just about everything we do is a choice, so I try to think long and hard before making a choice I'm not too sure about. If I'm going to choose it and then bitch about it, I need to make a different choice or live happily with the choice I'm making. It's frightening how many times that little rule pops up in my life.

Take Thanksgiving just a couple of years ago. For years and

years, Thanksgiving dinner was always at my mom's house. But as she and Dad got older, it somehow shifted and changed to my house. Truth be known, the first time I hosted the entire family, I think it was to show off a new house I had moved into. I was going to impress all of them.

There were to be seventeen for dinner and so, I spent all day cooking, preparing, making everything just right for a beautiful dinner. By the time everyone arrived in the late afternoon, I was tired and my back hurt from standing all day. Thanksgiving dinner is hectic because everything has to cook right up until the end, so I was running around trying to get it all done, shooing people out of my kitchen, and getting more stressed by the minute.

Then we sat down to a wonderful dinner, and it was all worth it. By the time the leftovers were put away and the pumpkin pie was gone, I was pleased with what I had been able to pull off. Then everyone started leaving, and I walked back into the kitchen to piles of dirty plates, pots and pans everywhere, and a sticky floor. Ugh!

Two hours later, while I was still doing dishes, I was bitching at all of them. *This is too much work. I'm never doing this again. Easy for them—they all come, eat, and leave. Look what I'm left with.* Bitch, bitch, bitch.

As I was getting started on the pots and pans, a little bell went off it my head. *Wait a minute, Dee Dee, you asked for this, you wanted to show off, you wanted to impress everybody, and you chose to have Thanksgiving here. You can't have it both ways. Stop bitching and get the job you asked for done.*

If you choose it …

●　　　●　　　●

Mom came out of treatment with a new life and often said those six weeks were the best thing that ever happened to her. Over the next six years, my dad's Alzheimer's got worse and worse, and she took care of him with love and patience that was truly amazing. None of us kids really knew how much she hid the terrible, difficult times she went through with him. I finally got a glimpse of what her life was like shortly before he died.

Mom really needed a break, so I offered to take care of him for a long weekend so she could travel to spend a few days with my youngest brother Jeff in New York.

Those three days were a big eye-opener for me. My dad had no idea who I was and was confused and angry. He yelled at me, hit me, pulled my hair, and tried to run away. I never told Mom how awful it was, because she knew. She'd been dealing with this insidious disease for nearly six years. She made sure his last years were as good as they could possibly be with the only person he still loved and recognized, his beloved redhead. To this day, I don't know how she did it. He died on June 12, 1993, at the age of eighty-three.

●   ●   ●

About six months after rehab, we knew Mom was going to be fine. I wanted to get started on my plans for a new life. I drove out to their house one Sunday morning to see how she would feel if I moved away. It was a much easier conversation that I was expecting.

She started it off. "Dee Dee, I know you were thinking about making some big changes in your life before I got sick. I want you to work on making those changes now. I know you stayed her for me, but I'm fine. What happened before will never happen again, and you need to have something to look forward to." She was looking healthier, with vibrant red hair and a glowing skin tone that showed her body was recovering from her previous bouts.

"Oh Mom, thank you for saying that. I just really feel like I need a different life than the one I'm living here. I don't know exactly what the looks like yet, but I'm grateful to know you understand."

She smiled. "I do understand; I want you to be happy again, and I think this is just what you need. Just don't move too far away."

"I promise."

I felt guilty leaving her with my dad's care, but she knew my life was not in a good place and was completely supportive of my choice. A few months later, while on a business trip to San Diego, I was sitting on a friend's deck early in the morning, drinking coffee, and watching the sun sparkle on the beautiful blue Pacific Ocean. After an hour of the smell of the ocean, the crystal-blue sky and the cry of the sea gulls, I made an instant decision. At nine o'clock on a Monday morning, I called my boss at the television station. "Good morning, Jeff. How is everything at the station?"

"Everything is good here," he replied. "Are you still in San Diego? You're driving back after your lunch meeting today, right?"

"Well, maybe not." I took a deep breath. "Jeff, I need to give you my thirty day notice. I need to make some changes, and I've decided to move to San Diego."

"What? Are you kidding?"

"I'm sorry Jeff, but I'm not kidding. I'll be back tomorrow

and we'll talk more. I won't leave until you have a new manager in place."

Just like that. After a few more minutes of conversation, I hung up and sat there terrified and excited about what I had done. *Holy cow, there's no going back now. San Diego, here I come.*

As I drove back to Phoenix the following day I spent the time planning my move and getting more excited about it as each mile passed. I was living in a nice apartment in Scottsdale with a roommate so I had to talk with her and give her enough notice to find someone to cover my part of the rent. First and foremost I had to get Amy's blessing. Amy was a senior in high school, happy in her life at Steve's, and had no plans to move back in with me after she graduated. But it was important to me that she was okay with me living 400 miles away. When I talked to her the following day her first question was "How close to the beach will you be?" She decided it was pretty cool that she could come to the beach whenever she wanted.

Two days after I told Lynn, my roommate, about my upcoming move, she came home after work and said, "Guess what? I'm going to go with you."

"Huh?"

"Yeah, I've really been thinking about it, so I talked to my boss. He can get me a transfer with the bank, so I gave him two weeks' notice."

Well, okay. That wasn't exactly what I had in mind, but I guess it was good. A few weeks later, she headed for San Diego to stay with a friend and start looking for place to rent. A week or so after that, I packed up all my furniture, had some friends help me drive over, and off we went. No job, no place to live, but what the heck. It was either incredibly stupid or brave, and probably a little of both.

●　　　●　　　●

The first year in San Diego was tough. We did find a great place to live in a great townhouse overlooking the ocean in Del Mar, but I really had trouble finding a job. The only thing I knew was radio or TV sales, but it seemed I was either over-qualified or under-qualified for every job I applied for.

Finally, during one interview, the sales manager said, "Look, you have a good resume and a good knowledge of radio, but nobody in San Diego wants to hire someone from another market. We would rather have someone who knows what's going on here, so you're probably beating your head against the wall."

I ended up taking a couple of other sales positions that didn't work out over the course of the next several months. I thought about going back home many times, but go back to what? More happy hours with the girls? I knew I needed to leave that life behind. I loved San Diego and was creating a much healthier life if I could just pay my bills. I still had not reached the place where I could truly believe in myself.

I couldn't seem to get a job in radio; I was depressed, questioning and doubting myself, and wondering what to do next. Nearly a year had gone by since I'd moved, and it just wasn't working. One day Lynn said to me, "You know, you're really not much fun to be around. Why don't you just move back?"

I was so mad and hurt at her comments. Who the hell did she think she was, and how dare she say I wasn't much fun to be around when I was in such turmoil and not sure if I could pay my bills or eat next week?

I gave myself a deadline until the end of the month to get something going or move back, and I think she was darn happy about that decision. I finally landed a radio job on the twenty-eight of the month and told her I'd be staying. I was mad at her for about ten years over those comments, but eventually I realized she was right. I'm sure I wasn't fun to be around and probably made her miserable. No one is much fun to be around when they whine and complain all the time and feel sorry for themselves. I've never forgotten what she said to me that day, and now I thank her. We are still friends. When I'm going through a bumpy spot in the road, I think of her comments and realize there is always a way up and out and whining doesn't help. If you choose it …

●   ●   ●

After a couple of years, I finally got grounded in San Diego and was enjoying my life. I was doing well in my sales job at the radio station and was happy. One of my clients at the station was an advertising agency, and in the later winter of 1990, I had a major presentation there to introduce a new promotion for one of their big clients. After the presentation, one of the executives asked me if I could stay for a bit and answer some additional questions. Chris was a good-looking man with thick black hair and a great smile. He was also pretty darn charming. I had a broken heart because of a relationship that had just ended with a man I thought was the love of my life. Turned out he wasn't, but I hadn't gotten over it yet. I really wasn't interested in meeting someone new.

Chris and I sat in the conference room and talked in more detail about some ideas I had for his client, and it was apparent there was some attraction on both sides. He was easy to talk to, funny, and flirtatious.

After a bit, he said, "Let's do some research and then meet again over coffee next week." In the next few weeks, we met for coffee, then dinner, and all of a sudden we were dating. I really tried to resist, but Chris was a nice guy and fun to be with. He filled a little part of the hole in my heart, and a relationship started. I was determined not to get involved, but he grew on me and it was good ... for quite a while.

We were together for ten years—probably three or four years longer than we should have been. We were not soul mates and were more like roommates those last few years. There were many things wrong with the relationship toward the end, but Chris and I came into each other's lives for a reason. He told me for years that I was the best thing that ever happened to him, that I helped loosen him up and taught him that he could not fight every battle. Life is too short. Chris finally taught me to believe in myself, that I had something to offer. All the men in my life tried to teach me that, but maybe I was just finally ready to hear it when Chris was there. He taught me that I could do anything I wanted, helped me start my first business, and supported me endlessly. We were not the best couple and not destined to be together forever, but I will always be grateful to Chris for the many gifts he gave me while we were together.

●   ●   ●

I never thought I had an entrepreneurial spirit. Hell, I spent most of my life thinking I wasn't good enough for whatever job I was doing. Starting my own business never entered my mind until Chris came into my life. He had worked for himself for many years and could not imagine any other way to live. It was the source of many disagreements. Most mornings I would get up at six, make coffee, and get ready for work. By eight I was in my home office working or preparing to go out for an appointment. And most mornings, Chris would get up at nine-thirty or ten, have a cup of coffee, and still be sitting on the couch reading the paper at noon. I didn't understand his work ethic, and it drove me crazy. On the other end, I was tired and ready for bed by ten o'clock at night, and Chris was just getting his steam up. Our schedules didn't mesh very well.

I was working for a software company selling software to radio stations and training sales people how to use it. I was happy with most of my job. Except...

This was 1991 and I didn't know much about computers. I had to learn real fast: kind of like learning a whole new language in about five minutes and then teaching it to other people. I was great at the training part, didn't really like the selling part because I couldn't understand the software, and was totally lost on the troubleshooting part. The owner of the company and I did not get along at all. I thought he was a male chauvinist pig, and he thought, well, I don't know what he thought but he didn't like me a bit.

About a year into this job, Chris and I decided to buy a house together. At the same time, I was going through contract renewal time with my company. They kept putting it off with one excuse after another. The company headquarters was in Chicago, and I was scheduled to go there in December for a sales meeting and contract renewal.

As I sat in front of my boss I asked, "Is there some reason the papers aren't ready for my contract renewal? It was supposed to be done by now. If there is a problem, then let's discuss it while I'm here."

"No, no, there's not a problem. We've just been very busy, and our HR department is just behind. Your paperwork should be ready in the next week or so."

"Well, good, because I'm looking for a house to buy in the next month or so, and I will need employment verification."

"Oh, we received the verification of employment papers from the mortgage company and signed them and sent them back. Everything is fine."

In the next few weeks, Chris and I found the house we wanted and were very excited about it. One Saturday morning in early February, we were on our way to show the house to my friend Carol, who was visiting from out of town. From there we were on our way to sign the final papers.

The phone rang as we were walking out the door. It was my boss. "Dee Dee, I'm sorry to bother you on a Saturday morning, but I need to let you know that we've decided not to renew your contract after all."

Oh my God! Are you kidding me? I'm walking out the door to spend all my savings and income on a house and I'm fired?

"What are you talking about?" I cried. "I asked you to your face less than a month ago, and you assured me I had a job this year. You knew I was buying a house. How could you do this?"

In his callous way that I'd never gotten used to, he replied, "Sorry, you are fired. Send back your computer and company materials. Your last day was yesterday."

Buckets of tears, hysteria, anger, nasty name-calling, and sheer terror! I was just in shock. Carol and Chris were watching me while I was on the phone and knew something was drastically wrong. When I hung up, I yelled, "I don't believe it! I'm fired!" I stomped around the house cussing and crying.

Chris tried to be sympathetic, but I was too upset to listen to him. After letting me rant and rave for twenty minutes or so, he said, "Honey, the realtor's waiting for us at the house. Let's just go show Carol the house."

Huh? "Chris, we can't buy that house! I don't have a job. I can't use my savings now. Are you crazy?"

Chris wasn't crazy, but he was persuasive as hell. Somehow he convinced me to go through with signing the papers anyway. I'm telling you, he was good. So Saturday afternoon I signed my life way, and Monday morning I filed for unemployment.

Just a few weeks earlier, I had landed a big contract with a radio station in Phoenix that I had been working on for months. Nancy, the station manager, was a powerhouse in the radio industry, and it was a coup to even get an appointment with her. When she finally signed the contract, she told me, "Look, I think the other company has a better product, but I think you are the best trainer. Because of you, I'm going to go with your company, but you better take care of my people."

Well, that was no problem. I was a good trainer; it was my favorite part of the job.

A few days after being fired, I jumped on a plane and off I went to see my former client to explain to her what had happened. It killed me to sit across from her desk and tell her I would not be able to handle her account as I had promised.

"Nancy, thanks for making time to see me. I know I wasn't scheduled to be here for a few more weeks, but something has happened and I wanted to tell you in person."

"Of course," she said. "I'm always happy to see you. But you don't look so happy. Why don't you just tell me what the problem is."

Boy, I hated to do this, but I had to get it over with. "I'm afraid there's been a change at the company, and I won't be handling your account after all."

"What?" she shouted. The ink was barely dry on the contract, and she was livid. She stood up, and I thought she was going to jump over the desk and grab me by the throat. "Dee Dee, you promised. You know the only reason I went with your company is because I want you as our trainer. Was this your plan all along just to get me to sign?"

Once I got her calmed down, I explained that I wasn't doing this voluntarily; I had not lied to her, nor had I just arbitrarily decided not to handle her account. "Nancy, I was fired!" I had to shout above her screeching.

"You what? No way. Are you kidding me? Let me get the SOB boss of yours on the phone. What's his number? Where is that contract? Tear it up."

I let her rant for a few minutes. Then I explained what had happened. It took a while for me to convince her that I had not sabotaged her and I was not any happier than she was. That's why I got on a plane, on my own dime, to sit in front of her and tell her instead of calling. We both said some very uncomplimentary things about my boss.

Then she said, "What are you going to do now?"

"I don't have a clue." I was still in shock and had no idea what my next step was.

"Well, why don't you start your own company?"

I laughed at her. "Doing what?"

"Do just what you're doing now, but do it on your own. You don't need that company. The radio stations subscribe to the information you need. You're the magic that turns it into something and teaches their people how to use it. Do it on your own. I'll be your first customer. What do you charge?"

She was going so fast I couldn't even keep up with her. But after a couple of hours of hammering it out together, I had my first client in a new business. I didn't have a clue what I was doing, but Nancy told me I'd figure it out. I was elated, overwhelmed, and terrified.

I called Chris that evening and told him all about my day and asked him what he thought. Of course he thought it was perfect because it was a lifestyle he was used to. He promised his support, and we talked for a long time about a name for my new business and all the details of how this might work.

The next day when I got home, Chris had a small white desk set up for me in the corner of the living room. Sitting on top of the desk was a stack of business cards and stationery with my new business name on them. He was a graphic designer, so once we had agreed on a name, he had gone to work (probably in the middle of the night) designing a logo and getting a few cards and sheets of letterhead printed. That was the sweetest, most supportive gesture. From that moment on, I was in business for myself. We celebrated with a romantic dinner and a bottle of champagne.

I woke up the next morning crying. *I don't know what I'm doing, I don't know the first thing about running a business, I don't know how to do what my first client wants, I don't know, I don't know, I don't know.*

To hear Chris tell it, I woke up for the next thirty days crying. I was sure I could not do this, and Chris was absolutely sure I could. So here's what I learned: Listen to the people who believe in you. They are probably right. Chris saw my strengths and abilities so much more clearly than I did. I couldn't get past the fear of failure long enough to see that just maybe I could do this.

That first month was ridiculously hard. I didn't know what I was doing. I was making this business up as I went along, and I had no idea whether I was doing it right. Poor Chris got so tired of my tears. Those first few weeks were hard; the first six months were hard; the first year was hard. I had to get appointments with managers or owners of radio stations and portray myself as this sales guru who could help their sales department sell more and reap the benefits of my wisdom. If I was lucky enough to get an audience, I then had to tell them I could do whatever they asked.

In one particular station, the owner really through me for a loop. "Well, Dee Dee, I don't think we need the kind of sales consulting you're offering. What I really need is someone to design brochures and collateral for the radio station. Do you offer those services?"

"Uh, sure." I said. "What exactly are you looking for?" In the back of my mind I'm thinking, *Take really good notes, Chris is a designer, he can do this for me or help me figure it out at least.*

"Great, how much do you charge?"

This was easy. Chris had helped me figure it out. I was going to charge forty dollars an hour for my services. Now all I had to do was say it. "Thirty dollars an hour," I blurted. He agreed, and all of a sudden I was a graphic designer.

But it was the best thing I have ever done for myself. I finally got to the point that I realized I could do anything I set my mind to. It took a lot of hard work, sweat, and tears. It was incredibly stressful. It changed my life forever in so many positive ways.

●   ●   ●

My company, Radio Sales Resource, was a busy and successful company for eight years. In 1998 there were big changes coming to the radio industry, and I knew my career would need to change as well. One of the last stations I worked for had asked me to hire some new salespeople, and that's how I met Kerry, who became my new business partner. I loved Kerry from the first interview and hired her immediately. After several months there, that station was sold, new management came in, and I knew it would end my relationship with the company. It ended Kerry's as well, as they fired all of the salespeople and brought in their own team.

I knew I needed to change my career but didn't know how. Kerry decided she really didn't want to be in radio and wanted to do something else as well. So we decided to help each other. We met for coffee every Wednesday morning for three months. It didn't take long for us to realize that we'd love to work together if we could just figure out what to do. We explored different ideas and very methodically worked on a plan that would suit both of us. We would list our strengths and weakness, where we complimented each other, and what skills we could bring to the table. We were problem solvers.

It became apparent that the consulting I had done for radio could be translated into any industry. Kerry had lots of management and event experience, and she was a star. She had been a professional ice skater, and she loved an audience! It wasn't long before we decided that together we were the perfect person, and Solutions Now was born. What did we do? Pretty much whatever we could find. We presented ourselves as management consultants, and within a few weeks we were getting work. We put on marathons, sales conferences, business meetings, and trade shows all over the country, doing project-based events that companies were happy to outsource.

When we started our business in 1998, Kerry told me that this was going to be a five-year plan for her. Her husband would retire then, and she was going to retire as well. Our business was great fun, and I loved every minute of it, but as we approached the four-year mark I knew I'd better start thinking about the next step.

●　　　●　　　●

I discovered my true passion when I happened to read an article in the newspaper one day about "life coaching." This was 2002, and coaching was a fairly new concept. I had never heard of it but was fascinated by the article, so I cut it out and saved it. A few months later, I was talking to my brother Ron, and during the conversation, he mentioned his life coach. (Yes, the brother who was a recovering alcoholic.) He obviously had found another path in his personal growth.

"Wait a minute. Life coach? You have a life coach? I just read an article about that recently, but I don't know anything about it. Tell me what that's all about."

He told me how this coach was helping him focus on his goals, overcome his weaknesses, and create a positive path that was helping him accomplish the things that were most important to him. He gave me his coach's phone number, and I called him to learn more. I was intrigued and curious.

They say when something occurs three times in your life, you really need to pay attention. So when a friend called two weeks later, I was a little dumbstruck. Kim called to tell me she was taking a class that night and didn't want to go alone, so would I go with her? I asked her to tell me what the class was about, and she said it was about life coaching. I told her that this was the third time the term life coach had popped up in the last couple of months, so I'd love to go with her. I really wanted to know more.

The class was at a local church and was led by a woman named Kathy and her husband Jim. They had been coaches for several years and taught us the basics of what coaching was all about: how it was not therapy but was a method to help people move forward with their goals and dreams. A personal coach is a person who works one on one to help someone figure out what they really wanted to achieve, what was holding them back, and how to overcome the obstacles and meet their goals. Having a coach is having someone to be accountable to but also to always have someone supporting you on whatever path you are on. Kathy and Jim did some live coaching demonstrations with a couple people from the audience and in a very short amount of time helped those people create a goal then clarify the steps needed to achieve it. It was great stuff.

I was hooked! After class I went up to talk to Kathy for a few minutes. I told her I was looking for a new career direction and was really interested in finding out more about this coaching thing. Could she help point me in the right direction to learn more? She gave me some materials to read, some websites to explore, and told me to do the research, and then if I was seriously interested to call her. She also told me that the first step to take was to hire a coach for myself so I could really understand the process. She gave me several names of coaches to talk with.

A few weeks later, I hired Kathy as my mentor coach and started studying. I had truly found my passion! I coached with

Kathy while I took classes for nearly a year as the event management business started winding down. I loved everything about it, but as the time drew near for me to leave the nest and start coaching on my own, my old insecurities started cropping up.

During a coaching session, Kathy said, "Dee Dee, you're ready. You've done everything you can to study and prepare. It's time for you to get a client."

"Yes, Kathy, but I'm not sure I understand how to use the Life Wheel. I'm not sure I can explain it properly to a client. I think I need to study a little more."

Next week's coaching session was just about the same.

"Dee Dee, you're ready. You need to get a client."

"Kathy, I need to ask you a few questions about the primary focus part of the process. I'm not sure I know it well enough to present it to a client. I think I need to learn a little more."

Week three: "Dee Dee, you need to get a client."

"Kathy, I don't think I'm ready. I just don't feel like a coach."

She laughed. "You're not a coach; you don't have a client! No more stalling! The only way to be a coach is to have a client and coach them. You will never 'feel' like a coach until you do that. Here's what you do. Find someone who knows what you're doing and offer to coach them for free for the first month. If they are happy with you at that point, they can hire you for your standard fee. Can you do that?"

"Yes," I sighed. "That's a good idea. I can do that."

I realized that I had fallen into my old pattern of believing I didn't know enough. But that's exactly what a coach is for, to push you a little bit harder than you'll push yourself.

The next time I talked to Kathy, I had my first client—one

who was to be my client for the next five years. Kathy was, and still is, one of the most amazing coaches I have ever met. I was so privileged that she chose to mentor and coach me for several years.

Coaching is still the greatest joy I've ever had in my career. There is tremendous satisfaction to witnessing and being a part of someone coming out of their shell, accomplishing more than they ever thought they could, and reaching goals they've put off for too long.

Through coaching, Jerry started his own business, Kim was promoted to sales manager, Tom learned to organize his life, and Jackie went back to school to get her nursing degree. It is an amazing privilege to be a part of someone else's journey. Embracing the tools of coaching is also what has helped me get through dark days and tough times.

D —— CHAPTER NINE

1991 Amy as an Adult

I remember that lesson I learned from my mom when I got married: either get on board or get out of the way. In 1991, when Amy told me she and Mark were getting married, I had some major flashbacks.

I was living in California and Amy was in Phoenix when she and Mark met. I knew they had been dating for several months, and I had the chance to meet him a few times when I had gone to visit. He was always on his best behavior around me, very polite and charming. He was in construction and worked with his dad, so he seemed to have his act together. Mark seemed like a nice enough guy, and he and Amy were dead set on getting married, so my pointing out that she was only twenty years old and "maybe she should wait" fell on deaf ears.

So I did what my mom did with me all those years ago. I wasn't going to talk her out of it; I could choose to be a part of it or not. I got involved. When Amy called me to tell me Mark has asked her to marry him, I got on a plane, flew to Phoenix, and helped her plan her wedding. We picked out flowers, a venue, the dress, all of it. It was a beautiful wedding, and we had a wonderful time.

In the first few years, they were very happy and worked on making a life together. Mark seemed to have steady work, and Amy had a job she liked, so they were heading toward Amy's goal. Ever since Beth died, all Amy ever wanted was to replace that beautiful little girl with one of her own. She didn't care about a career or anything else; she really just wanted to be a mom! So in early 1994, they were ecstatic to find out they were going to have a baby. When they called me to tell me the news, they decided to see what I was made of.

"Hi Mom. Guess what? You're going to be a grandmother."

A WHAT?

"Ha, ha, that's funny. You are kidding, aren't you?"

Mark got on the phone. "No Mom, we're not kidding. You better get used to being called Grandma."

"I'm not old enough!" I recited all the clichés: "I'm only forty-six years old. I'm way too young to be a grandma." But inside I was bubbling with joy. It was an amazing moment. I have since decided that grandparenting is without question the best job in the world. It's getting through parenting first that's harder than hell.

Seeing your daughter pregnant is kind of weird at first. We were all a little concerned that this might bring up some of her old medical issues, but she had a good pregnancy. I got a call one day in October that Amy had gone into labor and was in the hospital. I was still living in California and hated that I was so far away. This was my first grandchild. I had to get there.

I called Amy in the hospital, and she sounded bored to death.

She said, "Just fly in tomorrow. I don't think anything's going to happen for a while."

Steven was born later that evening. I got to the hospital early the next morning to meet my grandson. I had taken the first flight out of San Diego the next morning and was jumping out of my skin on my way to the hospital. As I walked into her room, I saw her laying there holding this tiny little bundle. This was my daughter, who wasn't supposed to live, who had overcome so much in her life, and now she got to experience the greatest joy on earth. I had huge tears in my eyes as I walked up to her. She held Steven up to me and said, "Mom, I'd like you to meet your grandson." What a beautiful moment to see my child with her first child.

When Amy went home from the hospital I stayed with them, held Steven as often as they'd let me, and helped Amy get settled into a routine. After a week I had to go back to work, but promised I'd be back soon. We talked every day, of course, so she could tell me all the miraculous things her child was doing. (He was a few weeks old; he wasn't doing much, but so what?)

●   ●   ●

In November, just five weeks after Steven was born, my phone rang very early on a Saturday morning with Amy on the other end. I could hardly understand her.

She said, "There's something wrong with Steven's leg; he's in the hospital. Can you come over for a few days?" She was crying and upset.

"Amy, you need to tell me more. What do you mean?"

"Mom, I don't know. The doctor said there is something wrong with his leg. He's in the hospital getting tests done and they may need to put a brace on his leg. I don't know any more than that; can you please come over here?"

Oh God, is my child reliving my life? How can this cycle repeat? A few hours later I was on a plane with my friend Carol holding me together. Carol was visiting me for my birthday and just jumped on the plane with me to help keep me sane while we made our way to Phoenix and the hospital.

We found Amy and went to see Steven in his little body brace. The bone in his right thigh wasn't growing straight, and they needed to stabilize it for a while. In order to do this, they needed to put is his leg in an enormous metal brace. The brace held his legs out at a ninety-degree angle, and he couldn't be moved much. It was so hard to see him lying there and watch Amy go through the same pain I had dealt with so many years ago with her.

As we sat in Steven's hospital room all day, I noticed several times that Amy still seemed to have a very large belly. After five weeks I thought her stomach should have been a little more back to normal, but I am smart enough to know better than to say anything about that to a new mom, so I kept my mouth shut. It bothered me, though. It didn't seem right.

That night, I told Amy and Mark to go home and get some sleep. I would stay with Steven all night in the hospital so they could be with him tomorrow. I settled into my cot next to his crib with so many thoughts and emotions going through me, it was impossible to sleep. I was worried about Steven and how difficult it was going to be to care for him with this brace. I was worried about Amy; I just couldn't let go of the feeling that something was wrong. And I was worried about Mark. His grandmother, who practically raised him, was in another hospital and not doing very well.

I tossed and turned and stared at the ceiling. Just after midnight, the nurse came into Steven's room and tapped me on the shoulder. She said Mark was on the phone for me, and it was important. My first thought was that his grandmother had taken a turn for the worse, so I quickly ran down the hall to the nurse's station to take the call.

"Mom, Amy's having terrible stomach pains. She can't even stand up straight, and I think I need to take her to the hospital. She says I'm overreacting, that it's just gas, but I'm worried. I think I need to take her."

Because of Amy's medical history, Mark had always been overly cautious when Amy was sick and tended to want to rush her to the hospital if she sneezed too hard. But this time I thought he was right.

"Mark, I didn't think her stomach looked right today. You get her to an emergency room." They went another hospital that was closer to them, and now we had Mark's grandma in one hospital, Steven in another, and Amy in yet another.

Amy was admitted to the hospital, and the next morning Mark came back to be with Steven while I drove across town to be with Amy. What a difficult time it was for everyone. We were all running from hospital to hospital looking after three different patients. It was so hard to see my little grandchild in one hospital and then worry so much about Amy.

Amy went through three days of testing and fasting. The doctors found a huge growth behind her uterus that had to be removed. They were very concerned about her because of the size of this growth and needed to cleanse her body for a few days so they could operate. When Amy had delivered Steven, they told her he was going to be a big baby, but he wasn't. Because this tumor was directly behind the uterus, it went undiscovered. That's the reason she was so big when she delivered and, of course, why she still looked pregnant. It all made sense now.

●   ●   ●

Everyone was exhausted and frazzled. For weeks, I spent my days going back and forth from Amy's hospital to Steven's. Mark would work as much as he could and then go to one hospital to visit his grandmother, stop by and see Steven at the second hospital, and then go see Amy in the third hospital. It would have been a whole lot easier if everyone was in one location!

The day before Thanksgiving, Amy had surgery to remove what the doctor lovingly called "Fred, the Ugly Brother." He even showed us a picture of the ten-pound tumor they removed from behind Amy's uterus. It looked like a really ugly, snotty soccer ball. Why they had not discovered this during Steven's birth, who knows? They didn't. They told us later that the tumor was not malignant but that they had to take it out whole so it would not break and spread toxins all through her body.

To do that required a twelve-inch incision that ran from her pubic bone to her chest. She was told she needed to stay in the hospital a few more days and then got strict instructions to be on bed rest; she was not to lift anything, including her baby, for eight weeks. Now that's fun for a new mother. They also had to remove one of her ovaries the tumor had killed, which I think was the worst part of all of it for her. We all knew that would definitely reduce her chances of future pregnancies.

Luckily, I had my radio consulting business at this time and could do a lot of my work by phone and computer, so it didn't matter where my home base was. Since Amy really couldn't take care of Steven when he got out of the hospital, we decided to have them come stay at my sister Shelley's house. I went back to California for a few days to pack and then came back prepared to stay a while. Everyone had jobs, and Amy couldn't be alone with the baby during the day, so we converted Shelley's living room to a nursery. We all settled in to the new makeshift rehab center.

Steven would be in the leg brace for several weeks, which meant handling him was challenging. It was awkward to figure out how to hold him or change him. Amy could only sit on the couch and look at him, could not do any of the things a new mother wants to do for her baby. I took care of him during the day, Shelley, her husband, or Mark would take care of his needs in the evening and night, and then we'd do it all again. I was going back and forth to San Diego every other weekend. Chris was holding down the fort for both of us in San Diego, and he would come to Phoenix to visit whenever he could get away. Mark was there in the evenings and other relatives were coming by to visit. It was a three-ring circus for eight weeks!

Now, there are several things wrong with this whole scenario. First, how hard must it have been for a brand-new mother to watch all of these other people love and care for her beautiful new baby? Every new mom needs to find her way and get comfortable with her child, and Amy did not have that chance until Steven was two months old. She must have bitten her tongue a hundred times a day as we all did things our way and not hers. We would try to be considerate and ask her how much to feed or if she thought his diaper should be changed, but most of the time we just did what we thought needed to be done. She never said anything except thank you, over and over again.

Then, there was the chaos of all these people now living in my sister's house, everybody doing things their own way, a screaming baby in the middle of the night, all of us trying not to step on each other's toes. My sister is messy, I'm neat and organized; she stays up late, I'm an early riser—there were just a million things that caused us all to bite our tongues, because this was the best situation we could think of. It was so incredibly generous of Shelley and Bob to open their house to this madness, but as a family, we barely survived. It's hard to live in someone else's house for any length of time. It's hard to have a bunch of people living in—and taking over—your house for any length of time. It wasn't easy for any of us.

For Amy first, but also for everyone's sanity, it was a very happy day when Mark packed them all up eight weeks later and drove them back to their own apartment. I was glad I could be there to help, and it was certainly hard to leave them on their own, but I've never been so happy to see the ocean as when I drove back to San Diego to stay.

●　　●　　●

Mark and Amy's life finally settled in, and they got to be a family. Steven was an adorable and happy baby, and I had become so attached to him during those first few months of his life. I was still visiting Phoenix as often as I could just to see his beautiful smile. For a long time, things were relatively normal—no more hospitals or craziness. Steven continued to grow and thrive as a toddler, and life was good.

In the spring of 1997, Mark and Amy decided they needed a change and announced that they were moving to San Diego. Mark was always restless, always thought the grass was greener on the other side. I thought it was great that they were moving closer to me, but even then, San Diego was a more expensive place to live than Phoenix, so I had my doubts. They asked if they could stay with us until they found a place of their own, so again we were one big happy family: Chris and me, plus Amy, Mark and Steven camping out in our converted garage. A few days after they moved in, Amy found out she was pregnant, so that made life even more fun. She discovered that only having one ovary didn't slow her down a bit. She said they had just stopped birth control a month previously, thinking it would take a long time to get pregnant with one ovary. Hah!

Two weeks turned into two months, and just as we were all about ready to kill each other, they found an apartment and life settled back down. It was great to be so close to Amy again, and of course having my grandchild close was the best thing that could have happened. On September 16, 1998, Kyle was born, and I had my second grandson.

By 1999 it was more than apparent that my relationship with Chris had turned into a platonic one. We grew further and further apart. Chris brought many good things to my life, but we would never agree on some important issues—little things like his earning an income. Chris had always worked for himself, but he didn't always do it successfully, at least in my eyes. He was not driven by money, he was driven by doing what he wanted when he wanted to do it, whether he made much money or not. We fought about it a lot, because in those last few years, paying the mortgage became more and more my responsibility.

One night in October, we had a loud and stupid fight. We were standing in the hallway yelling at each other about something. At one point, Chris yelled at the top of his lungs, "Stop trying to change me! You're always trying to change me!" This had been our fight—on both sides—for a long time. If only I could change him and if only he could change me, we would be great.

I'd heard those words come out of his mouth a hundred times, but this time I felt like I truly heard them for the first time. I just stopped in my tracks and quietly said, "You know what? You're right. I am trying to change you, and I can't do that anymore."

Chris stormed out of the house, and I sat on the couch, finally letting my feelings come to the surface. I didn't want Chris like he was, and he really didn't want me unless I could change to be more like him. Our differences were good up to a point. I know I brought a lot to Chris's life, and I will always be grateful for what he brought to mine. But we could no longer respect those differences enough to live together peacefully.

He came back home a couple of hours later, and I was still sitting on the couch. "Come sit down," I patted the couch. "We need to talk. " We were still sitting there when dawn broke.

I think Chris would have stayed together a lot longer if I hadn't initiated that conversation, but it wasn't working, and we both knew it. We decided to put the house up for sale, split the proceeds, and go our separate ways. When the house sold a few months later, Chris took his money, bought a trailer, and traveled around the country for several months until he ran out of money.

In February of 2000, I invested in rental property and moved into one of the houses on that property. That was the difference between us. He wasn't wrong and I wasn't right—we were just not on the same journey. We parted on good terms, although all my friends joked that I couldn't get rid of him. Before he left on his trip, he rented a room from me. I finally had to kick him out after three months so I could get my life started on my own! He has since found someone else to love, and I hope he is happy. Remarkably, after more than ten years apart, he continues to be Grandpa Chris to Amy's boys.

●　　　●　　　●

One of my best memories from my time with Chris was Yosemite National Park in California. Thank you, Chris, for introducing me to that incredible place of beauty and nature. It was one of his favorite places to visit, and he was surprised that I had never been, so we went on our first camping trip to Yosemite. It was love at first sight. It is breathtaking and now one of my favorite places on earth. We went every year for five years and took some of our closest friends with us because it is just one of those places that needs to be shared.

One of those trips wasn't quite as much fun as the rest. It was in June of 1997, and we were packing to go on our annual Yosemite trip. The evening before we left, Chris and I were in front of the house getting the camping gear loaded into our car. It was just about dusk when Amy pulled up in front of the house. I thought that was strange; she usually called before she came over, and she knew we were leaving very early in the morning. As she got out of the car I yelled, "Hi honey! Did you come to help?" But then I looked up and saw the look on her face—a look I had never seen before. It quickly registered that something was drastically wrong.

As she stomped up the sidewalk she glared at me. "Stop packing. We need to talk. Now."

"Amy, you're scaring me. What's wrong?"

"Don't worry, nobody's hurt, but we need to talk, and you

probably don't want to have this conversation in your front yard."
Holy crap. I couldn't figure out what I had done to make her so mad, but it was obvious her wrath was aimed straight at me.

"Okay, let's go in the back. Just tell me what's wrong."

Chris gave me a questioning look but I just shrugged and told him we were going to the back patio to talk. We walked through the house and sat down on the back patio. She just sat there fuming and couldn't even get words out. I was scared and kept asking what was wrong.

"Are you pregnant? Is that why you're upset?"

She just stared at me and said, "This is not about my ovaries; it's about yours."

Whoa! Huh? I didn't get it at first, but warning bells started going off in my head.

Tears started running down her cheeks as she shouted, "How could you lie to me all these years?" Sirens started blaring in my head. She was shaking she was so mad. She stood up and leaned over the table. "How could you not tell me I have a brother? Why wouldn't you tell me that?"

Oh no. Oh crap. I was so stunned that I didn't know what to say. I had to choose my words carefully here, but I didn't know the right words. I sat there as tears started running down my face as well. "Oh, Amy, I am so sorry."

She stopped me before I could get any further. "Don't you dare lie to me. Do I have a brother?"

I lifted my head at looked at her. "Yes, Amy you do, but I can explain."

"Explain? How can you explain?"

I had worried for so long that this might happen. How could she possibly have found out? Steve and I agreed that unless we knew how to find him, the last thing Amy needed in her life was another loss. We had never found the right time to tell her about the brother she could never have. She was more furious than I had ever seen her and hurt beyond words. My biggest question was, how did she find this out?

A couple of years after Steve and I had divorced, he married again and they had another daughter, Amy's half-sister Jessica. Steve and his wife lived in northern California most of the time they were married.

Jessica was ten years younger than Amy, and they had become close friends. She was visiting Mark and Amy the week we were preparing to go to Yosemite. Amy had gone to bed the night before, and Mark and Jessica stayed up playing video games and evidently doing a little drinking. They got into a discussion about families, and Jessica said something to Mark like, "I wonder why Amy never talks about her brother."

Mark looked at her like she had two heads. "Amy doesn't have a brother."

Jess said, "Well, my mom told me she did."

Mark, thinking Amy had been keeping a secret from him, went in the bedroom and woke her up, yelling. "Why in the world haven't you ever told me you have a brother? I can't believe you'd keep something like that from me."

Amy thought they were both crazy and yelled back, "What the hell are you talking about?"

That started a conversation that lasted well into the night and the next day. Amy stewed about it all day and eventually called Jessica's mom to get more information from her. Then she headed straight to my house. Yikes, what a mess! How could I possibly explain this secret so that it would make sense to her?

That evening Amy sat there waiting for answers. I slowly started trying to make her understand this whole chapter of my life she knew nothing about. Finding the right place to start was the hardest part. "Amy, this is a long story. Please just listen to me, and I will tell you the truth, I promise."

She had no sympathy for me. "The truth would be nice, Mom."

Ouch. Over the next two hours, I told her the entire story of getting pregnant and giving our child up for adoption. I tried to explain our reasons for protecting her. "Amy, your dad and I have talked about this a thousand times. We both agreed not to tell you because there's nothing we can do to find him. We've tried."

"You haven't tried hard enough. Why would you ever quit trying?"

"It's not that easy, Amy. We have looked for him." It sounded lame even to me as I tried to get her to understand. She asked a hundred questions but would not let her anger go. I couldn't blame her. Listening to myself, it didn't sound so great either.

As I answered her questions over and over again, she suddenly looked up. "I can't believe my father was a part of this. Maybe he'll give me better answers that you have."

We went into the house to call her dad so she could yell at him for a while. "Hi Steve, I'm sorry to call you this late in the evening, but Amy's here and she's very upset and wants to talk to you. She's fine, but she just found out she has a brother, and she's pretty upset."

There was silence on the other end of the phone, so I brought him up to date on how she'd found out and that she and I had been talking for most of the evening. He was just as speechless as I had been earlier.

"We need to tell her the truth. I have been trying to tell her the reasons we have kept this from her all these years, but she needs to hear it from you."

Then the three of us talked for another two hours. Steve explained that if she needed to blame someone, he was as big a part of this secret as I was. He tried to make her understand that he and I had a commitment to never tell her unless we both agreed. He told her how, over the years, there were many times when one of us wanted to look for her brother but the other was not ready. Just in the last few years, we had done hours and hours of research to see if there was a way to track him down, but we kept hitting dead ends. In Arizona adoption records were sealed, and there was no way to get to them.

Steve supported me and took responsibility for his part in our deception. When we were through talking, she was a little calmer, but when she left, she told me she was glad I was going out of town and didn't want to talk to me until we returned. What a miserable trip that one was. It was such a beautiful and serene place, but this time I couldn't enjoy much of it. I worried about Amy and about our relationship. I wasn't sure she was ever going to forgive me for this one.

When we got back from Yosemite a week later, Amy was still pretty icy toward me, but we talked more, and after a few weeks, the wedge between us disappeared. What took place of the anger, however, was her determination to find her brother. She was positive we had not been thorough enough.

●　　　●　　　●

As life moved on, Amy and Mark and the boys seemed to be happy, and their family was keeping her busy. In the summer of

2000, Amy found out she was pregnant again (maybe it's a good thing she didn't have two ovaries) and wanted to have a little girl more than anything in the world. She adored her boys, but she had wanted a girl for almost thirty years. When she found out she was to have her third boy, it broke her heart at first, but as soon as Alex arrived, on April 28, 2001, she, and everyone else, fell in love with this beautiful baby boy. Final score: Boys 3, Girls 0.

●　　　●　　　●

For the next few years, life was good. I loved my home in San Diego, and my business was doing well. My coaching career was really starting to grow, and I was expanding my services to include seminars and workshops for businesses.

One night in early spring, Mark and Amy came over for dinner with some news to share. Amy's dad, Steve, was living in Phoenix and running a swimming pool company. The company was growing, and he offered Mark a superintendent's job. Mark had been in construction all his life and thought that this was not an opportunity they should pass up. They would be able to buy a house, and he could learn a business that would always be growing in Arizona. Mark was very excited—there's that green grass again—and I knew it was probably a good thing for them but oh, would it be hard to be away from them and my grandkids. I bit my tongue and had a quick little talk with myself before I spoke out loud.

"Wow, this really sounds like a good opportunity. It's so expensive to live in San Diego. This could really be a good thing for your family, so I'm happy for you." Amy knew it was hard for me to get those words out. I didn't want them to move away, but I couldn't keep them here. When Amy told me her dad was going to help them buy a house, I knew the deal was sealed and I just had to get used to it.

Over the next few weeks, Amy spent hours and hours working on me. "Mom, come on, why don't you move back too? Houses are more affordable; you'll be close to us." Blah, blah, blah.

I told her I had no interest in moving back to Arizona. I'd been in San Diego fifteen years at that point, and did not want to move back to Phoenix. Period! Actually, I had been thinking about looking at property somewhere else. I eventually wanted to work less and live somewhere that was more affordable than Southern California. However, moving back to Phoenix was not my first thought.

Then Amy went straight for the jugular. "You're not going to be able to see your grandkids all the time." Oh, that's so true, and so unfair. I adored those boys, and I loved being their grandmother. So Amy started her campaign, and she was relentless; every time we talked, she'd tell me all the benefits of moving to Phoenix.

The seed was planted, and my brain starting ticking. I realized that if I were clever, I could buy a house in Arizona without selling my house with the rental properties in California. I could hang on to my San Diego property, move to Arizona, and go back and forth. If I could afford to keep one of the little apartments open and furnished, then we could all go back whenever we wanted. Oh, the wheels were turning now.

Plus, Mom was past eighty, and I felt I really should spend time near her while she was still active and healthy. My brother and sister lived there. I could see my grandkids … Okay, I think we've got something. It took me a few months to come to grips with leaving San Diego, but this was a good plan, financially practical, and it kept me near my kids, grandkids, and family.

Amy and Mark started making their plans. Mark needed to be in Arizona around the first of May, and Amy would wait until the boys were out of school to move. Amy's dad helped them find a house to buy, and Mark got started learning his new job. I decided I would go whenever I found a house I wanted to buy, got some things settled, and got renters in San Diego. I wasn't in any hurry to get back there in the summer. Then I got the phone call that let me know my move back to Phoenix was exactly what I should be doing.

CHAPTER TEN

2003 Full Circle

Back to the beginning …

My first child was born in 1966, and except for a few moments in the hospital, I had not seen him for nearly thirty-eight years. The first few years after our son was born and put up for adoption, Steve and I talked about him often, but as the years went by, the conversations become fewer and farther between. Later we talked every year on his birthday and always had the same conversation: should we look for him this year? We were truly committed to our decision and vowed not to interfere in his life and create havoc and heartache for the people who were raising him. We also had agreed that once he was an adult, we may try to find out about him, but only if both of us agreed. Neither of us would go against the other's wishes.

Once Amy found out about her brother, though, she was determined to find him. After a couple of years of internet searches, she understood that maybe this wouldn't be so easy and realized she may never know her brother. We had periodically gone on all the websites designed for adopted children to find their parents and vice versa. You register on those sites, and if the other party is registered as well, you will be connected. Once Amy knew everything, we had also contacted a private detective, but he told us that without a name, it would be virtually impossible.

"In Arizona, adoption records are sealed for ninety-nine years," he said. "The only way to get them is the black market; pay someone in county records a lot of money under the table to look at the records."

We seriously thought about doing that but never could bring ourselves to go that route. Not to mention the fact that we wouldn't know how to go about such a plan. We were conflicted about whether to look for him, but for Amy's sake, we made several attempts.

So time went on, and there were times we seriously looked and times we didn't. As I got older, I think I settled into the fact that I would never know, but it was difficult. I had reasons to pursue finding him: I just wanted to know if he was okay. I wanted to know if he'd had a good life, if he was healthy, if he had a loving family and what kind of person he turned out to be. I never wanted to interfere in his life. I just wanted to take a peek at it.

I remember when Amy asked if Bethany could come back from heaven for just a while so she could make sure she was okay. I think that's how I felt about finding my son. I didn't need to keep him; I just needed to know. The other reason, of course, was for Amy. She lost a sister and now knew that she had a brother that she might never meet. It must have felt almost like another loss of a sibling, so I can understand why Amy was so driven about this.

●   ●   ●

On Mother's Day in 2003, Steve called me. I was still living in San Diego, and he was in Phoenix. Amy and Mark were preparing to move back to Phoenix in the next several weeks, and I planned to move back sometime over the summer. When I picked up the phone, I was a little surprised to hear Amy's dad. Steve said, "Nothing's wrong."

Why else would he be calling me then?

He went on, "There's an article in the paper this morning that caught my attention, and I think you should see it. It looks as if there may be a way for us to contact our son."

I almost started hyperventilating. "What? Tell me what it says!" He read some of the article, which told of a program in Arizona that that, upon request, allowed a mediator to open the adoption records and find the name of the adoptee. Then if that person was willing, he would be told that his birth parents were looking for him. If he agreed to be contacted, the mediator set it up; if not, it was over.

Wow! This was big news to digest.

"Steve, I hardly know what to say. I don't know if I'm scared or excited, but it's time. I'm ready if you are, and we know Amy is. We have to move forward with this and at least try, don't you think?"

"Yes," he replied. "I agree. I'm scared too, but I think we have to do this. I'm going to email you the article right now. Call me after you've read it, and we'll decide what to do."

This was startling, and I didn't know what to think our how to feel. Our son was an adult. He could decide whether to meet us, but this was our first real chance to find out what happened to him. So, shaking inside, I said yes, let's go forward. We have to pursue this. The question was: do we tell Amy now, or wait and see if there is any result? This could turn into nothing. I think Steve and I had both learned our lesson. All of this took place while Mark and Amy were in the midst of moving back to Phoenix. Mark was already there, and Amy was only a few weeks away from packing up the truck.

Steve called a few times during the week to tell me he had filled out the paperwork and started the process. The next Friday afternoon, I was at Amy's house to baby-sit while she ran some errands. Just as she was ready to walk out the door, her father called and asked to talk to me. Amy knew something must be up and that she better hang around to find out what was going on.

When I took the phone, his first words were, "You better sit down."

We were out on her back patio, and the only thing there was a folding chair. I walked over and sat down and took a deep breath. Amy was staring at me. My insides were jumping all over the place.

Then, after a pause I heard the most amazing words: "They found our son."

Those were words I never thought I'd hear. I was dumbfounded. Amy said I turned white as a sheet, and she thought I was going to pass out. She came over and tried to listen in as Steve went on to tell me that the mediator had contacted our son's adoptive father to let him know that his son's birth parents were trying to contact him. Steve actually spoke to Roy—the adoptive father—and learned that our son's name was Dale and that he lived in Phoenix. He had lived in Phoenix his entire life. We had always been within just a few miles of each other.

From what I heard later, Dale's father was not too thrilled to get the phone call from the mediator. I imagine he felt threatened by this news out of the blue, but he agreed to pass on the message to his son. When Dale got the information that both his birth parents were looking for him, he immediately contacted the mediator and told her he was willing to move forward. A few days later, the mediator arranged a phone meeting between Dale and Steve. Steve would then call me, and if it went well, Dale and Amy and I would have a phone conference soon after.

On Wednesday evening, Steve and Dale spoke to each other for the first time. Amy and I were so nervous we could hardly sit still. She came to my house to wait, and we just paced the floor. I had so many emotions and thoughts colliding. I was so excited and so afraid at the same time.

Would he hate us? Would he understand? Did he want to know us? Would this be a beginning or another end?

My strongest emotion was fear. I think over all the years, fear is what kept me from trying harder to find him. *What if he hates me?* I paced the floor and wrung my hands. I felt like I could vomit at any minute. I was barely holding back tears and trying to think positively, but it wasn't easy. Amy was excited. She had no fears, because she's not the one who had abandoned her child. She just knew she had a brother she wanted to finally meet.

After their phone call, Steve called Amy and me in San Diego and told us what a great call he and Dale had. He said, "We had a great conversation. Dale is friendly and easy to talk to."

Amy grabbed the phone and put it on speaker so we both could talk. Steve told us that he and Dale had talked for an hour or so, filling each other in on stories of their lives. We bombarded Steve with questions and made him repeat the conversation again and again. We found out that Dale was a firefighter, and he was engaged to Rachel, who had two children, Kayla, eleven, and Spencer, five, from a previous marriage. Dale and Rachel had been college sweethearts who lost touch and then found each other again after seventeen years apart. Dale talked about how close he was to his mom. She had been battling cancer for a very long time and was sick again. He talked about his grandfather, who died of cancer several years ago. Dale and Rachel, Steve and his wife Pat all planned to meet for dinner on Sunday night.

The next morning Steve emailed me some photos of Dale. When I opened the first photo, it all finally hit me. I thought I was looking at a picture of my father in his thirties. I was floored. There was no doubt that this was my son. There were a couple other pictures of Dale, his fiancé, and her two children all dressed up at Easter. I wept off and on most of the day and kept going back to my computer to look at the photos over and over again. It was so emotional to actually see a picture of him. It made it real. I was going to meet my son.

●   ●   ●

As fate would have it, we found out much later, Dale had seen the same article in the newspaper, had cut it out and laid it on his desk. He too decided maybe it was time to know who is birth parents were. Events were syncing up in all of our lives.

Steve told us that Dale had no anger toward us and was anxious to meet his birth family. So then the strangest thing happened: my son called. Oh my God! I thought I was going to throw up, I was so nervous. Amy was there with me when I answered the phone. I felt so awkward, fumbling around the words. "Hello, Dale. It's nice to meet you, kind of, I mean by phone, at least." Ugh, that was lame.

He chuckled. "I'm really happy to meet you too, kind of. Hopefully, we'll really meet very soon."

Steve was right. Dale just jumped into conversation, telling us about his job and about Rachel and his family. It was just like having a conversation with someone you haven't seen in a long time. After we got started, we just caught up in the most natural way.

Steve had already filled him in on details—that his birth parents had eventually married, that he had a full-blooded sister, and one that he had lost. He had always known he was adopted and knew the reasons why. His parents were totally supportive of him meeting us. Well, his dad had reservations in the beginning, but his mom was amazing.

Amy let him know that she and Mark were in the process of moving back to Phoenix and that she would be there in just a few days, so they made arrangements to meet. I was so envious. I was moving sometime over the summer, but I had renters moving in San Diego and didn't have a place to live yet in Phoenix, so it was just not feasible for me to go for a while. It was frustrating to be the last one to meet him, but I kept telling myself I had waited thirty-seven years; I could handle a few more weeks.

So everyone got to know Dale except me. So unfair! It took longer than I'd planned to get things settled in San Diego and find a house to buy in Phoenix. I just couldn't stand it any longer! I finally told Amy, "I can't wait anymore, so I'm going to fly to Phoenix on the Fourth of July weekend." (Yes, another Fourth of July life-changing event)!

"Great," she said. "I'll make arrangements with Dad and Dale for all of us to get together." The reunion would be on Saturday at Steve's house and would include Steve and his wife Pat; Amy and her boys; Dale his fiancé and her children; and me—the only stranger. And oh yeah, Dale's adoptive mom.

Dale had asked me over the phone if it would be all right. "My mom really wants to meet you. Is it okay if she comes over for a little while on Saturday?"

That kind of took me by surprise. "Really? Uh, sure, I guess that's good. Are you sure she won't be uncomfortable?"

"When I told her I was going to meet you, she told me she has always wanted to be able to thank you in person for giving her a son. It would really mean a lot to her."

I didn't see that coming. I was a little overwhelmed but, of course, agreed. It was going to be quite a day.

I flew in to Phoenix on Friday night, and Mom picked me up from the airport. We went back to her house and talked long into the night. She had been very apprehensive and uncomfortable about this whole reunion thing. When I first told her we had found Dale, she was not overjoyed and tried to talk me out of meeting him. I couldn't believe she felt that way.

"Mom, how do you think I could possibly not meet my son?"

It was obvious she was concerned. "Dee Dee, what if this doesn't go well? You know, not all of these adoption stories turn out well."

"I know, Mom, but we've already talked to him. He's a good person, and I cannot take this away from Amy. I have to do this no matter how it turns out. What are you so afraid of?"

She took my hands in hers. "You've had so much pain in your life. I can't stand the thought that this might bring you more.

And Amy doesn't need any more loss in hers. I'm just afraid you're going to get your heart broken."

"Mom, I know you're worried for me, and I love you, but I have to go through with this. I have to close the circle."

●　　　●　　　●

That Saturday morning I was an absolute mess! I woke up and was crying within five minutes. I couldn't hold it together for more than about fifteen minutes before the tears would start streaming again. That did nothing to help my mom's anxiety, but I just couldn't keep it together. I was a nervous wreck.

I was supposed to be over at Steve's by one o'clock in the afternoon and ended up going over before noon because I just couldn't sit still. I hoped maybe Steve and Amy could get me to calm down. Before I got in the car, Kellie, my dearest friend, called from California to see how I was doing and wish me well. Of course, as soon as I heard her voice, I started crying again. I told her there was nothing wrong, I didn't know why, but I was just an emotional wreck and really needed to stop this so I didn't meet Dale with a big red nose and puffy eyes!

She said, "Sweetie, you always leak when you're nervous."

I had to laugh. "I do?"

"Always. You always have. It's just nerves. You'll be fine."

I did feel a little bit better, but of course cried again because she knew me well enough and cared enough to call me on that special day.

Just after noon, I arrived at Steve's house and finally got fairly calm. I thought I had the tears under control. But as one o'clock drew near, I started getting nervous and shaky again. I was standing in the kitchen with Amy and Mark when the doorbell rang. I was instantly paralyzed. The tears sprang out of my eyes, I started shaking, and I couldn't move. Could not move. At all. Could not put one foot in front of the other. I heard voices out in the living room, but I couldn't get there. Amy and Mark came into the kitchen to see what was keeping me. I just stood there crying.

Amy gently took my by hand and said, "Come on, Mom, it's time to meet your son."

She and Mark each took an arm and started guiding me to the door into the living room and had to help me walk all the way. As I rounded the corner into the living room, I looked up. There, standing in the doorway, was this big man with dark hair and dark eyes and a smile on his face. I just stood still, feeling like I might faint. He took two big steps across the room and wrapped his arms around me while I sobbed.

This sweet man just kept his arms around me and whispered in my ear, "It's okay. I won't let go until you're ready. You just let me know."

I don't think I could ever find the words to truly express how that moment felt. I had spent so many years shoving my thoughts and emotions away and now here he was, with his arms wrapped around me. It seemed like the world just melted away. I didn't see anything or hear another sound. My head was buried in his shoulder, and I was flooding his shirt with tears. My nose was running, and his poor shirt got that too. I was trembling and my knees were weak; I think Dale was really holding me up. I didn't want it to end. It was one of the most amazing moments of my life. The baby I had held for a few minutes and given away so long ago was now this man, holding on to me and trying to soothe and comfort me. This was my son.

After several minutes I could finally stand on my own, and it occurred to me that I hadn't even really looked at him. I backed away so I could see his face.

He smiled at me. "Are you okay?"

And then all these people came over to meet me. He introduced his fiancé and her two children and then there were more hugs and more tears. Boy, they must have thought I was the crazy lady. Well, okay I was. We finally all collected ourselves and sat down to talk. I have no idea what we talked about.

Plus, he had brought an album of his baby pictures. We got to see pictures of him growing up, which, of course brought on more tears. We could see the resemblance to Steve; in some teenage pictures, he looked just like him. We laughed at the pictures from the seventies with his long hair. In a picture of him as a little boy in his baseball uniform, he looked like one of Amy's boys. In the pictures where he had a mustache, he looked like my dad. It was wonderful and painful all at the same time.

We discovered Dale had lived in west Phoenix all his life. We told each other the stories of our lives, and we overwhelmed him trying to fill him in on family members and who belonged to whom, and to this day he still doesn't get it all straight. I have a big family, Steve has a big family, and poor Dale had to try to put all these people in the right slots and remember all those names. I've thought many times how overwhelmed he was that first year. So many people to meet. He only had one brother, but there were dozens and dozens of us. Poor guy had no idea what he was getting into.

A little later that afternoon, his mom arrived. She walked up and put her arms around me. "I've always wanted to able to thank you for the incredible gift you gave me." As we hugged and talked, the dam broke again, and there I was causing another flood.

Dale walked over to me and asked if I was okay. He said, "This is supposed to be a happy day. I hate seeing you so upset."

I tried to explain to him that I had emotions erupting that I had been stuffing for nearly thirty-eight years, and they were just going to keep erupting for a while.

Dale's mom and I talked for a long time that afternoon. She had the most incredibly generous spirit. She just couldn't see any reason why Dale having more family and more people to love him could possibly be a bad thing. She was battling cancer for about the fourth time and said to me, "I am so happy that Dale has found you. I've been fighting this cancer for a long time, and I'm tired. If the cancer finally wins, it will give me a lot of joy and peace to know that Dale will have family with him when I'm gone."

I wondered if I could ever be that generous. I was at a loss for words. We just sat in silence holding hands.

I didn't want that day to ever end, but of course it did, and I was exhausted. I went back to my mother's house and told her about all the amazing things that had happened. She was relieved to see my joy at finally knowing who he was. When we finally found our son, I told Steve that I truly did not have expectations about what this would look like in the future, that I honestly just wanted to know about him. If nothing further developed, I would be okay with that. I truly meant that. If for some reason I could never see him again, I wouldn't like it, but I could live with it. I got the opportunity to meet my son, and I really didn't need more.

● ● ●

Slowly, week by week, our relationship did grow, and Dale wanted to meet his new family. Be careful what you wish for; he had no idea how involved that would be. I have three brothers and a sister, Steve has a brother and a sister, and we both have lots of nieces and nephews and other relatives who were finding out about this new person.

Most of the people in my life didn't know anything about Dale. In those first few weeks, it was awkward to tell people about him. When I had the girls, I naturally told people I had two children when asked. After Beth died, I had to get into the habit of saying I had one child. Now when people ask, I can say I have a son and a daughter, but it was awkward in the beginning.

Little by little, we introduced Dale and Rachel and their family to members to our family. We'd get together on a weekend and explain each new group: "Now this is my sister and her husband Bob and their son Scott," or: "This is Steve's brother, and his wife …"

It was so overwhelming for Dale to try to keep track of all these people and who they belonged to. Thank goodness he had his wife Rachel there to help keep him organized and remind him which family member he was meeting that day. He still has to ask once in a while. I tried to keep in mind what this must have been like from his side. We just got to meet Dale and Rachel and her two children. He got to meet dozens and dozens of relatives.

We'd be at a family gathering, and he'd come over to me and whisper, "Now who is that guy in the corner, and who does he belong to?" Maybe the most amazing thing was for me to stand in a room full of people—family I'd known all my life—and have this stranger there with us. Amy's husband got a real kick out of walking over to me and saying: "Hi, Mom. Look over there—that's your son and daughter talking to each other." It would just hit me all over again that this person was my son. For a very long time, I would have to almost pinch myself to realize that this nice man who stopped by for coffee is not just some new person I know.

He's my son.

One morning, a few days after our first meeting, my phone rang. When I answered, the voice on the other end of the phone said: "Hi, Mom." The *male* voice on the other end of the phone said that, not my daughter's voice—my son's. I had never heard those words from him, and I was speechless.

After a few moments, he said, "Are you there? Hello?" And then: "Oh, man, are you crying again?" He has no idea how many tears of joy I cried whenever he called.

After I moved to Phoenix and got settled in my new house, Dale wanted me to meet some of the people he worked with so asked me to come down to the fire station. One of the guys walked in, and Dale said, "Hey Joe, I want you to meet my mom." I immediately got all flushed and embarrassed and emotional.

Joe said, "Wow, I've heard all about you. It's great to finally meet you."

Later I pulled Dale aside. "You know, you don't have to call me Mom. I don't expect that at all, and I'm fine with you just calling me Dee Dee."

He shook his head. "No, I've told everyone I know that I've met my mom, and that's what I'll call you if it's okay."

"Yes, it's okay."

Then there was the first time I called over to the house and

Rachel answered the phone. She yelled, "Dale, your mom's on the phone."

He answered, "Which one?"

●   ●   ●

A few months after we met Dale, I was going through my journal one day looking for something. I'm not very good about keeping a journal and certainly wish I'd been better at it as I call up these memories, but every once in a while I would write something important in it. This is what I found that day; words that were written just over a year before we met:

Thursday, April 4, 2002
A letter to my son,

Happy thirty-sixth birthday, wherever you are. I hope you are having a good life and that you are happy. I still remember holding you for a few moments that morning thirty-six years ago before I gave you to someone else to love. I have never regretted my decision. I still deeply believe that it was the right thing to do at that time. But I wonder so often how different my life would have been had I made another choice. I will never know. I hope somehow, deep in your heart, you know the decision was made out of love for you. I hope your life was filled with family and love and that you have not spent all these years hating me. It is my deepest fear but something that I can do nothing about. If I regret anything it is that you don't know your sister and that she doesn't know you.

I would never interfere with your life, but I would love the chance to take a peek at it and know what you are. I would like Amy to have a brother. It would mean so much to her. I would like to be able to tell you why I didn't keep you and look in your eyes and see that you understand.

I would like to know if you've ever tried to find me and to explain to you why I haven't tried too hard to find you. I don't know now if I'll ever have that chance, so I just pray and choose to believe that you would understand and forgive me.

If I am really honest, I would tell you that the strongest driving force in not looking harder for you is my deep fear that you would hate me for my choices. That would be too difficult to bear, unless through it all you would have a sister and she would have a brother. That would make it worthwhile. I guess I'm selfish that I let my fear lead my way.

We have looked for you—your father, your sister and me—but I think maybe it is not meant to be. So if we never meet, if I never get to see your face, I hope you will somehow know that you were loved and thought of throughout my life. I am blessed to have a daughter who is still here, I was blessed to have a daughter who is gone, and I was blessed to have you to give to a family who wanted you so much.

Happy birthday,
Mom

Then, unbelievably, a little more than a year later, I handed a copy of that letter to him.

●   ●   ●

In October of 2003, I danced with my son at his wedding. His sister was a bridesmaid. There were a lot more people on their invitation list than they had originally intended; a whole new family of relatives he never knew he had. I finally met his dad, Roy, and we got to know each other a little. His fears were put away and he welcomed us into their lives.

That night, other couples swirled on the dance floor, the band played, and the reception bubbled around us. In his tuxedo, Dale walked over to my table, a smile on his face. He looked happy, fulfilled in a life that I couldn't have imagined for him—one I couldn't have given him.

"May I have the last dance?" He bowed gracefully.

Tears streamed down my face—again. This handsome young man, my son, was back in my life. I cried through the entire dance.

EPILOGUE

All of this happened nearly ten years ago. It was taken me a very long time to finally get all this down on paper. It is not easy to go back and pull up memories and feelings from so long ago; many of them I buried in a very deep place. As Bethany's thirty-seventh birthday approaches, I have pulled these pages out and gone into those deep, dark places to once again try to bring them to the surface. Each year as August approaches, Amy asks me about Beth. Her memories are only from the stories I've told her, and she wants to know more. Dale and I talked again recently about the amazing story of our reunion and even those memories from ten years ago start to fade a little, so it's all here—the good, the bad and the ugly.

We all still live in Phoenix—the whole big, mixed-up family. After the chaos and overwhelm of the first year with Dale, it has calmed down, and we have found a place in each other's lives. Dale and Rachel now have two more children, Collin and Brooke, plus Rachel's two, so they are always busy. I now have seven grandchildren! I'll never forget the day Dale and Rachel came to my house to tell me I was going to be a grandmother again, something I thought would never happen.

I have always felt that since we invaded Dale's life, it was up to him to decide how much he wants us in it. We talk on the phone or see each other often. We celebrate birthdays and holidays together, and I try to be a part of my grandchildren's lives. It is good. Still, even after all these years, I am a little unsure of my place in his life, but we are family.

Amy and Mark are no longer married. Mark decided it was just too much responsibility and left nearly eight years ago. Steven is now eighteen and has just enlisted in the Navy. He's a great young man with a solid plan for his future. Amy is raising Kyle and Alex on her own, and it's never easy. But she showed her strength and character early in her life, and she does what she has to do to take care of her boys. I never forget how blessed I am to have her in my life.

Sadly, Dale's adoptive mom, Pat, passed away in December of 2008. Roy, his adoptive father, now lives in California with his new wife, Leona.

My mom became ill in late 2008 and had a long and difficult two years until she passed away in October of 2010. I spent a lot of time with her those last two years, and I'm still amazed at how much I miss her every day. In the last fifteen years of her life, Mom became an accomplished artist, something that her grandson Dale inherited. He spent a good deal of time with her in the eight years they had together, and they found a very special bond through their art. Every once in a while he incorporates a little bit of her in one of his wood pieces, and it is evident that even though they only knew each other a short while, she's still very much a part of him.

My life has not always been easy, but I have finally learned that tough times are not forever. There is more joy out there if you just stay strong a little bit longer until it shows up. It's all about the journey, and mine has definitely been a roller coaster. I have lived through tragedy and unbelievable sadness. I have been blessed and have found strength I didn't know I had. I have had incredible joy, and I have experienced miracles. I have laughed more than I have cried. I have learned that much of what life brings depends on the choices you make and just maybe, if you believe and hold on long enough, you may experience the miracle of your journey coming full circle.